AF270330

Presented to

____

on the occasion of

____

by

____

on

____

Queen of Apostles

PRAYER BOOK

Queen *of* Apostles

PRAYER BOOK

A Catholic Treasury

Compiled and edited by
Mary Mark Wickenhiser, FSP

Pauline
BOOKS & MEDIA

Boston

Nihil Obstat:

Reverend Thomas W. Buckley, S.T.D., S.S.L.

Imprimatur:

✠ Seán Cardinal O'Malley, O.F.M. Cap.

Archbishop of Boston

February 25, 2014

ISBN-10: 0-8198-6209-6

ISBN-13: 978-0-8198-6209-9

Cover design by Rosana Usselmann

Third edition, 2014

Published by Pauline Books & Media, 50 Saint Pauls Avenue, Boston, MA 02130–3491

Printed in China

www.pauline.org

Pauline Books & Media is the publishing house of the Daughters of St. Paul, an international congregation of women religious serving the Church with the communications media.

2 3 4 5 6 7 8 9   28 27 26 25 24

To Mary, Mother of God's people, Teacher, and Queen of Apostles, who introduces us to her Son and guides our journey of faith.

May she show us how to best fulfill in our lives what her Son desires for us.

And may she share with us the joy she experienced—a joy that came not from a life without pain, but from a heartfelt trust and fervent hope in her Son, her Savior and ours.

CONTENTS

DAILY PRAYERS

Morning Prayers

The Sign of the Cross

In the name of the Father, and of the Son, and of the Holy Spirit. Amen.

The Morning Offering

O Jesus, through the Immaculate Heart of Mary, I offer you all my prayers, works, joys, and sufferings of this day, for the intentions of your Sacred Heart, in union with the holy Sacrifice of the Mass throughout the world, in reparation for my sins, for the intentions of my loved ones, and for the general intention recommended this month by the Holy Father.

Adoration and Praise

I adore you, my God, and I love you with all my heart. I thank you for having created me, made me a

Christian, and sustained me through the night. I offer you my actions of this day: grant that they all may be according to your will and for your greater glory. Preserve me from sin and all evil today. May your grace be always with me and with all whom I love. Amen.

The Angelus

℣. The angel spoke God's message to Mary,
℟. and she conceived of the Holy Spirit.
Hail Mary . . .

℣. "I am the lowly servant of the Lord:
℟. "Let it be done to me according to your word."
Hail Mary . . .

℣. And the Word became flesh
℟. and lived among us.
Hail Mary . . .

℣. Pray for us, holy Mother of God,
℟. that we may become worthy of the promises of Christ.

Let us pray.

Lord,
fill our hearts with your grace:

once, through the message of an angel
you revealed to us the incarnation of your Son;
now through his suffering and death
lead us to the glory of his resurrection.
We ask this through Christ our Lord. Amen.

The Regina Caeli

(Prayed during the Easter Season instead of the Angelus.)

Queen of heaven rejoice, alleluia.
For Christ, your Son and Son of God,
has risen as he said, alleluia.
Pray to God for us, alleluia.

℣. Rejoice and be glad, O Virgin Mary, alleluia.
℟. For the Lord has truly risen, alleluia.

Let us pray.

God of life,
you have given joy to the world
by the resurrection of your Son, our Lord Jesus
    Christ.
Through the prayers of his Mother, the Virgin
    Mary,
bring us to the happiness of eternal life.
We ask this through Christ our Lord.
Amen.

The Lord's Prayer

Our Father, who art in heaven, hallowed be thy name; thy kingdom come; thy will be done on earth as it is in heaven. Give us this day our daily bread, and forgive us our trespasses, as we forgive those who trespass against us, and lead us not into temptation, but deliver us from evil. Amen.

Hail Mary

Hail Mary, full of grace, the Lord is with you. Blessed are you among women, and blessed is the fruit of your womb, Jesus. Holy Mary, Mother of God, pray for us sinners, now and at the hour of our death. Amen.

Glory

Glory to the Father, and to the Son, and to the
  Holy Spirit,
as it was in the beginning, is now, and will be
  forever. Amen.

An Act of Faith

O my God, I firmly believe that you are one God in three divine Persons: Father, Son, and Holy Spirit;

I believe that your divine Son became man and died for our sins, and that he will come to judge the living and the dead. I believe these and all the truths which the holy Catholic Church teaches, because you have revealed them, who can neither deceive nor be deceived.

An Act of Hope

O my God, relying on your infinite goodness and promises, I hope to obtain pardon of my sins, the help of your grace, and life everlasting, through the merits of Jesus Christ, my Lord and Redeemer.

An Act of Love

O my God, I love you above all things, with my whole heart and soul, because you are all-good and worthy of all love. I love my neighbor as myself for the love of you. I forgive all who have injured me, and I ask pardon of all whom I have injured.

Prayer of Entrustment

Dear and loving Mother Mary, keep your hand
upon me this day;
guard my mind, my heart, and my senses, that I
may not commit sin.
Make my thoughts, affections, words, and
actions holy, so that I may be pleasing to
you and to your divine Son, Jesus, and attain
heaven with you.
Jesus and Mary, give me your holy blessing:
In the name of the Father,
and of the Son, and of the Holy Spirit.
Amen.

Evening Prayers

Adoration and Praise

I adore you, my God, and I love you with all my heart. I thank you for having created me, made me a Christian, and sustained me throughout this day. Forgive me my failings and sins, and accept whatever good I may have done today. Take care of me while I sleep and deliver me from all danger. May your grace be with me always and with all whom I love. Amen.

Bless the Lord (Psalm 103)

Bless the Lord, my soul;
    all my being, bless his holy name.
Bless the Lord, my soul,
    and let not all his kindness be forgotten;
he forgives all your guilt;
    he heals all your infirmities;
he rescues your life from the grave;

he crowns you with loving kindness and
tender love;
he bestows fulfilling goodness upon your years.
The LORD is compassionate and gracious,
slow to anger and rich in loving kindness.
Glory to the Father . . .

For a selection of other Psalms, see page 239.

Examination of Conscience

Take a few moments for a brief examination of conscience (see page 286). Reflect on the ways God acted in your life today, how you responded to his invitations to think, speak, and act in a more Christ-like manner, and in what ways you would like to be a more faithful disciple tomorrow.

An Act of Contrition

O my God, I am heartily sorry for having offended you, and I detest all my sins, because of your just punishments, but most of all because they offend you, my God, who are all-good and deserving of all my love. I firmly resolve, with the help of your grace, to sin no more and to avoid the near occasions of sin.

(Or any other prayer to express sorrow for sin.)

Psalm 23

The Lord is my shepherd;
    nothing do I want.
He makes me lie down in verdant pastures,
    he guides me along soothing streams.
He refreshes my soul.
        He leads me along paths of righteousness
        for the sake of his name.
Even though I walk in the dark valley I fear
            no evil,
        because you are with me.
        Your rod and your staff give me courage.
You spread the table before me in the face of
            my foes;
        you have anointed my head with oil;
        my cup overflows.
May only contentment and loving kindness
        be with me all the days of my life,
        and may I dwell in the house of the Lord for
            years to come.
Glory to the Father . . .

Hail, Holy Queen

Hail, holy Queen, Mother of mercy, our life, our sweetness, and our hope! To you we cry, poor banished children of Eve; to you we send up our sighs, mourning and weeping in this valley of tears. Turn then, most gracious advocate, your eyes of mercy toward us, and after this our exile, show unto us the blessed fruit of your womb, Jesus. O clement, O loving, O sweet Virgin Mary.

To the Guardian Angel

Angel of God, my guardian dear, to whom God's love entrusts me here, ever this night be at my side, to light and guard, to rule and guide. Amen.

For the Faithful Departed

Eternal rest grant to them, Lord, and let perpetual light shine upon them.

May they rest in peace. Amen.

Invocation for a Holy Death

Jesus, Mary, and Joseph, I give you my heart and
my soul.

Jesus, Mary, and Joseph, assist me in the hour of
my death.

Jesus, Mary, and Joseph, let me die in peace with
you.

BLESSINGS FOR MEALS

Grace Before Meals

Bless us, O Lord, and these your gifts, which we are about to receive from your bounty, through Christ our Lord. Amen.

Good and gracious God, nourish our bodies with this food, our hearts with your love, and our spirits with your truth. Through Christ our Lord. Amen.

Grace After Meals

We give you thanks for all your gifts, O loving God, you who live and reign forever. Amen.

Heavenly Father, we thank you for the food we have received through your goodness. Keep us mindful of all the blessings that come into our lives from you, and give us grateful hearts so that we may be blessings to others. Amen.

PRAYERS TO THE
HOLY TRINITY

The Apostles' Creed

I believe in God, the Father almighty,
Creator of heaven and earth,
and in Jesus Christ, his only Son, our Lord,
who was conceived by the Holy Spirit,
born of the Virgin Mary, suffered under Pontius
    Pilate,
was crucified, died, and was buried;
he descended into hell; on the third day he rose
    again from the dead;
he ascended into heaven, and is seated at the
    right hand of God, the Father almighty;
from there he will come to judge the living and
    the dead.
I believe in the Holy Spirit, the holy catholic
    Church,
the communion of saints, the forgiveness of sins,
the resurrection of the body, and life everlasting.
    Amen.

Te Deum

(A Christian hymn of praise dating back to the fourth century.)

We praise you, O God; we acknowledge you to
be the Lord.
All the earth worships you, the everlasting
Father.
To you all the angels, the heavens, and all the
Powers,
the Cherubim and Seraphim cry out without
ceasing:
Holy, holy, holy Lord God of hosts!
The majesty of your glory fills the heavens and
the earth.
The glorious band of apostles,
the great company of prophets,
the white-robed army of martyrs praise you.
Throughout the world the holy Church extols
you:
the Father, whose glory is without measure,
your true and only Son, worthy of total
adoration,
and the Holy Spirit, the Paraclete.
You, O Christ, are the King of glory.
You are the eternal Son of the Father.

You did not spurn a virgin's womb to redeem
    mankind.
You overcame death, and opened the kingdom of
    heaven
to all those who believe.
Now you are seated at the right hand of God, in
    the glory of the Father.
We believe that you will come again as our
    judge.
Help your servants, whom you have redeemed
    with your precious blood.
Number them among your saints in everlasting
    glory.
Save your people, O Lord, and bless your inheri-
    tance.
Govern them, and keep them safe forever.
Through each day we bless you
and praise your name forever; indeed, forever
    and ever.
Grant, O Lord, to keep us without sin this day.
Have mercy on us, O Lord; have mercy on us.
Let your mercy be upon us, O Lord, as we place
    our trust in you.
In your mercy, O Lord, I have trusted; let not my
    trust be in vain.

℣. Let us bless the Father, the Son, and the Holy Spirit.

℟. Let us praise and exalt him forever.

℣. Blessed are you, O Lord, in the firmament of heaven.

℟. Worthy to be praised, glorified, and exalted above all forever.

Let us pray.

O God, your mercy is limitless and the treasury of your goodness is boundless. We give thanks to you for the gifts we have received and look to you for the answer to our every petition. Continue your kindness, forsake us not, and prepare us for the reward to come. Through Christ, our Lord. Amen.

The Divine Praises

Blessed be God.
Blessed be his holy name.
Blessed be Jesus Christ, true God and true man.
Blessed be the name of Jesus.
Blessed be his most Sacred Heart.
Blessed be his most precious blood.
Blessed be Jesus in the most Holy Sacrament of the altar.

Blessed be the Holy Spirit, the Paraclete.
Blessed be the great Mother of God, Mary most
holy.
Blessed be her holy and Immaculate Conception.
Blessed be her glorious Assumption.
Blessed be the name of Mary, Virgin and
Mother.
Blessed be Saint Joseph, her most chaste spouse.
Blessed be God in his angels and in his saints.

Consecration to the Most Holy Trinity

O Divine Trinity, Father, Son, and Holy Spirit, present and active in the Church and in the depths of my soul, I adore you, I thank you, I love you. And through the hands of Mary most holy, I give myself entirely to you for life and for eternity.

To you, heavenly Father, I offer and give myself to be consecrated as your child.

To you, Jesus Master, I offer and give myself to be consecrated as your brother/sister and disciple.

To you, Holy Spirit, I offer and give myself to be consecrated as "a living temple" to be blessed and sanctified.

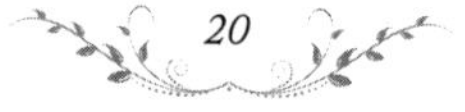

O Mary, Mother of the Church and my Mother, teach me to live through the liturgy and the sacraments in ever more intimate union with the three divine Persons, so that my whole life may be a "glory to the Father, to the Son, and to the Holy Spirit." Amen.

Blessed James Alberione

Doxology to the Holy Trinity

Holy God, Holy Mighty One, Holy Immortal
   One, have mercy on us.
To you be praise, to you be glory, to you be
   thanksgiving now and for ages unending,
   O Blessed Trinity. Amen.

PRAYERS TO THE

HOLY SPIRIT

Prayer of Consecration

Divine Holy Spirit,
eternal Love of the Father and of the Son,
I adore you, I thank you, I love you,
and I ask you pardon for all the times
I have grieved you.
Descend with many graces during
the ordination of bishops and priests,
during the consecration of men and women
    religious,
during the reception of Confirmation by all the
    faithful.
Be light, holiness, and zeal.
Spirit of Truth, sanctify my mind, imagination,
    and memory;
enlighten me.
May I know Jesus Christ our Master
and understand his Gospel and the teachings of
    the Church.
Increase in me the gifts of wisdom, knowledge,
    understanding, and counsel.
Spirit of Holiness, guide me in your will,
sustain me in the observance of the command-
    ments,

in the fulfillment of the responsibilities of my
    life's calling.
Grant me the gifts of fortitude and holy fear
    of God.
Life-giving Spirit, sanctify my heart.
Nourish and increase the divine life in me.
Grant me the gift of holiness. Amen.

Blessed James Alberione

Prayer for Enlightenment

℣. Come, Holy Spirit, fill the hearts of your
    faithful.

℟. And kindle in them the fire of your love.

℣. Send forth your spirit and they shall be
    created.

℟. And you shall renew the face of the earth.

Let us pray.

O God, you have instructed the hearts of the
faithful by the light of the Holy Spirit; grant us in
the same Spirit to be truly wise and ever to rejoice in
his consolation. Through Christ our Lord. Amen.

To the Spirit of Pentecost

Holy Spirit, Spirit of Pentecost,
help me to clarify what is ambiguous,
to give warmth to what is indifferent,
and to enlighten what is obscure,
so that I may be for the world
a true and generous witness of Christ's love,
because no one can live without love. Amen.

Saint John Paul II

To the Spirit of Love

Come, Holy Spirit.
Come, Mighty Spirit.
Spirit of love and wisdom.
Spirit of light and power.
You help us in our weakness.
Come, fill our inmost being.
Come, Holy Spirit, come to us.
Transform us so that our hearts may be
a new creation of your love.
Guide us with your wisdom and love,
and let the radiance of your light
renew the face of the earth. Amen.

Carlo Recalcati, SSP

Come, Spirit, Our Creator

(Veni Creator Spiritus)

O Spirit and our Creator,
come and dwell in every soul you have made.
Bring to birth the flame of love
in these hearts which belong to you.
You are our consoler and our certain hope,
you are the gift of God the Most High.
You are the source of our life and the fire of love,
anointing sent us from above.
You are the reflection of the Father's love,
the fulfillment of his promise, too.
You stir in us the gift of grace,
putting your wisdom upon our lips.
Your seven gifts give to your flock.
Come, fill our hearts with your own love.
You are our everlasting joy.
You are the power which can never fail.
From danger save us, Mighty One,
and help us follow Christ the Son.
Through darkness, pain, and through every loss
our hope is certain, trusting in you.
Most Holy Trinity on high,
the Father, Son, and Spirit one.

Your people praise you with all their heart,
longing for heaven, O vision blest!

For an Outpouring of the Holy Spirit

Holy Spirit, Lord and Giver of life,
you who came down upon the Apostles
in a mighty wind and with fire,
who filled the house where they were and
gave them the gift of tongues
to proclaim the wonders of God,
come down now upon me also.
Fill me with yourself,
and make of me a temple wherein you dwell.
Open my lips to proclaim your praise,
to ask your guidance,
and to declare your love.
Holy Light, divine Fire, eternal Might,
enlighten my mind to know you,
inflame my heart to love you,
strengthen my will to seek and find you.
Be for me
the living and life-giving Breath of God,
the very air I breathe,
and the only sky in which my spirit soars.

Prayer for Holiness of Life

> Breathe in me, O Holy Spirit,
> that my thoughts may all be holy.
> Act in me, O Holy Spirit,
> that my work, too, may be holy.
> Draw my heart, O Holy Spirit,
> that I may love only what is holy.
> Strengthen me, O Holy Spirit,
> that I may defend all that is holy.
> Guard me, O Holy Spirit,
> that I always may be holy.

Saint Augustine

Before Reading Sacred Scripture

> Open my heart, O Holy Spirit, to receive your
> inspired word.
> Grant me wisdom to understand what you want
> to teach me,
> and strength of will to follow wherever you lead.

After Reading Sacred Scripture

I thank you, Holy Spirit, for the word you have spoken to me through the treasure of the Scripture.

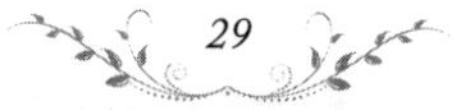

Make these words a living reality in my life—a constant guide, a lamp for my feet and a light to my path. Amen.

Litany of the Holy Spirit

(For private use.)

Lord, have mercy on us.
Christ, have mercy on us.
Lord, have mercy on us.

God, the Father of heaven,	*have mercy on us.*
God the Son, Redeemer of the world,	*save us.*
God the Holy Spirit,	*sanctify us.*
Holy Trinity, one God,	*hear us.*
Holy Spirit, proceeding from the Father and the Son,	*have mercy on us.*
Holy Spirit, co-equal with the Father and the Son,	*have mercy on us.*
Holy Spirit, Comforter,	*have mercy on us.*
Holy Spirit, Sanctifier,	*have mercy on us.*
Holy Spirit, Paraclete,	*have mercy on us.*
Promise of God the Father,	*have mercy on us.*
Gift of God Most High,	*have mercy on us.*
Ray of heavenly light,	*have mercy on us.*

Author of all good,   *have mercy on us.*

Source of Living Water,   *have mercy on us.*

Consuming Fire,   *have mercy on us.*

Burning love,   *have mercy on us.*

Spirit who in the beginning
   moved over the waters,   *have mercy on us.*

Spirit who overshadowed Mary
   that she might conceive and
   give birth to Jesus,   *have mercy on us.*

Spirit who descended upon Jesus
   at his baptism,   *have mercy on us.*

Spirit who on the day of Pentecost
   rested upon the disciples in the
   form of tongues of fire,   *have mercy on us.*

Spirit who at our baptism gives
   us birth into the divine life,   *have mercy on us.*

Spirit who dwells in us,   *have mercy on us.*

Spirit who builds, animates,
   and sanctifies the Church,   *have mercy on us.*

Spirit of truth,   *have mercy on us.*

Spirit of wisdom and
   understanding,   *have mercy on us.*

Spirit of right judgment and
   courage,   *have mercy on us.*

Spirit of knowledge and of love,   *have mercy on us.*
Spirit of reverence,   *have mercy on us.*
Spirit of grace and prayer,   *have mercy on us.*
Spirit of peace and joy,   *have mercy on us.*
Spirit of patience and goodness,   *have mercy on us.*
Spirit of modesty and chastity,   *have mercy on us.*
Spirit of adoption of the
   children of God,   *have mercy on us.*

That you enlighten our minds
   with holy inspiration,   *we beseech you, hear us.*
That you inflame our hearts
   with the fire of your love,   *we beseech you, hear us.*
That you open to us the
   treasures of your grace,   *we beseech you, hear us.*
That you guide us along
   the path to holiness of life, *we beseech you, hear us.*
That you teach us how to pray
   with humility and trust,   *we beseech you, hear us.*
That you clothe us with love
   toward all peoples,   *we beseech you, hear us.*
That you fill us with loathing
   for sin and evil,   *we beseech you, hear us.*
That you direct us in the
   practice of good,   *we beseech you, hear us.*

That you grant us the grace to
 persevere in virtue
 throughout our life,   *we beseech you, hear us.*
That at the end of our life
 here on earth, you will be
 our everlasting reward,   *we beseech you, hear us.*

Lamb of God, you take away the sins of the world,
 spare us, O Lord.

Lamb of God, you take away the sins of the world,
 hear us, O Lord.

Lamb of God, you take away the sins of the world,
 have mercy on us.

℣. Come, Holy Spirit, fill the hearts of your
 faithful.

℟. And kindle in them the fire of your love.

Let us pray.

Merciful Father, grant that your divine Spirit may enlighten, inflame, and cleanse our hearts. May he penetrate us with his heavenly dew and make us fruitful in good works, through Jesus Christ our Lord. Amen.

PRAYERS TO

JESUS CHRIST

Devotions to Jesus Master, Way, Truth, and Life

Invocations to Jesus Master

Jesus Master, sanctify my mind and increase my
faith.

Jesus, teaching in the Church, draw everyone to
yourself.

Jesus Master, deliver me from error, empty
thoughts, and spiritual blindness.

Jesus, Way between the Father and us, I offer
you everything and await all from you.

Jesus, Way of sanctity, help me to imitate you
faithfully.

Jesus Way, grant that I may respond wholeheartedly to the Father's call to holiness.

Jesus Life, live in me, so that I may live in you.

Jesus Life, do not permit anything to separate
me from you.

Jesus Life, grant that I may live eternally in the
joy of your love.
Jesus Truth, may you shine in the world
through me.
Jesus Way, may I faithfully mirror your example
for others.
Jesus Life, may I be a channel of your grace and
consolation to others.

Blessed James Alberione

Prayer for Light

Give me your light, Divine Master,
to know you and to know myself.
Your wisdom is infinite.
You gave me light for my eyes.
You gave me the light of reason.
You gave me the light of faith.
And still you will give me the light of glory,
where I can contemplate you for eternity in
heaven.
Therefore, I beg you to give me the grace to use
well
my sight, my reason, and my faith.

Blessed James Alberione

That Christ Be Formed in Me

Master, your life traces out the path I want to follow; your teachings strengthen and illuminate my steps. Your grace renews and sustains me along the path to heaven. You are the perfect Master; you teach and give example and encouragement to us, the disciples who follow you.

Master, you have words of eternal life. Substitute my mind and my thoughts with yours. You enlighten every man and woman, for you are Truth itself; I want only to be guided by your teachings, to judge according to your criteria, to think as you think. Live in my mind, O Jesus Truth.

Your life is way, the only secure, true, sublime way. In the stable, at Nazareth, on Calvary, you trace out for us the divine path of love for the Father and love of neighbor to the point of total sacrifice. Make me know your way; may I always follow in your foot-steps. Jesus, I want only what you want. Establish your will in place of mine.

Replace my heart with yours. Replace my love of God, of self, and of neighbor with your love. Replace my sinful human life with your divine life. So that your life will ever grow in me, I will give every care to the reception of Holy Communion, participation at holy Mass, the visit to the Blessed Sacrament, and devotion to the passion. May this life be manifest in works; may the life of Christ be manifest in our body (see 2 Cor 4:10) as it was in Saint Paul's, who said: "Christ lives in me" (Gal 2:20). Live in me, O Jesus, eternal and substantial life.

Blessed James Alberione

Chaplet to Jesus, Divine Master

1. We Adore You, Jesus Truth

Jesus, Divine Master, we adore you as the Word Incarnate sent by the Father to teach us life-giving truths. You alone have words of eternal life. We believe in you and the teachings of the Church, and we pray that your Word may enlighten our minds. Master, show us the treasures of your wisdom; let us know the Father; make us your true disciples. Increase our faith so that we may reach eternal life in heaven.

2. We Adore You, Jesus Way

Jesus, Divine Master, we adore you as the Beloved of the Father, the sole Way to him.

We contemplate you throughout your earthly life. We want to follow your teachings and example,

treating everyone with love and respect. Draw us to yourself, so that by following in your footsteps, we may seek only your will. Increase hope in us and the desire to be similar to you, so that we may rejoice to hear your words: "Just as you did it to one of the least of these . . . you did it to me" (see Mt 25:34, 40).

3. Live in Us, Jesus Life

Jesus, Divine Master, we adore you as the only-begotten Son of God, who came on earth to give abundant life to humanity. We thank you because by your death on the cross, you give us life through Baptism and you nourish us in the Eucharist and in the other sacraments. Live in us, O Jesus, with the outpouring of the Holy Spirit, so that we may love you with our whole mind, strength, and heart, and love our neighbor as ourselves for love of you. Increase charity in us, so that one day we may all be united with you in the eternal happiness of heaven.

4. We Adore You Living in the Church

Jesus, Divine Master, we adore you living in the Church, the Mystical Body of Christ, through which you bring us to eternal life. We thank you for having

joined us together as members of the Church, in which you continue to be for humanity the Way, the Truth, and the Life. We ask that those who do not believe may receive the gift of faith, that those who are separated may be brought into full communion, and that all people be united in faith, in a common hope, and in charity. Assist the Church and its leaders; sustain the People of God. Lord Jesus, our wish is yours: that there be one fold under one Shepherd, so that we may all be together in heaven.

5. Jesus, May We Radiate You

Jesus, Divine Master, we adore you with the angels who sang the reasons for your Incarnation: glory to God and peace to all people. We thank you for having called us to share in your saving mission. Enkindle in us your flame of love for God and for all humanity. Live in us so that we may radiate you through our prayer, suffering, and work, as well as by word, example, and deed. Send good laborers into your harvest. Come, Master and Lord! Teach and reign over all.

Blessed James Alberione

To Read Sacred Scripture

Jesus, Divine Master,
you have words of eternal life.
I believe, O Lord and Truth; increase my faith.
I love you with all my strength, O Lord and
    Way;
grant that I may always follow your command-
    ments.
I pray to you, O Lord and Life.
I adore you, I praise you,
I beseech you, and I thank you
for the gift of Sacred Scripture.
With Mary, I want to remember and preserve
    your words in my mind
and ponder them in my heart.
Jesus Master, Way and Truth and Life,
have mercy on us.

Blessed James Alberione

Devotions to the Sacred Heart of Jesus

Prayer of Trust

O Heart of love, I place all my trust in you. Although I fear my own weakness, I hope all things from your goodness.

Saint Margaret Mary

Act of Reparation

Most loving Jesus, whose immeasurable love for humanity is too often returned with negligence and disrespect, we wish to make a special act of homage in reparation for the indifference and pain to which your loving heart is subjected.

We ask pardon for our part in this ill-treatment and affirm our desire to do penance for our personal sins and for the sins of those who have strayed from

the path to salvation and who no longer follow your law of love and mercy.

It is our intention to offer the satisfaction that you once made on the cross to your Father and that you renew daily on our altars at Holy Mass. We offer this in union with Mary, your Mother, and all the saints in heaven. With the help of your grace, we promise to make reparation, as much as we are able, by deepening our faith and observing your law of charity. We promise to do all we can to proclaim your love to others through our witness of holiness and Christian commitment.

Most loving Jesus, through the intercession of the Blessed Virgin Mary, our model in atonement, accept our offering of this act of reparation. Keep us steadfast in your love until the day you bring us home to the happiness of heaven, where you, with the Father and the Holy Spirit, live and reign, God forever and ever. Amen.

Prayer for Healing

Almighty and eternal God, healer of those who trust in you, through the merits of Jesus Christ, your Son, hear my prayer for [*name*]. In your tender mercy, restore her/him to spiritual and/or bodily health,

that she/he may give you thanks, praise your name, and proclaim your wondrous love to all. Amen.

Prayer of Praise and Thanksgiving

It is fitting for us to praise and thank God for the blessings he has given us and the graces he continues to bestow.

Lord Jesus, I praise and glorify you for all the blessings you have bestowed on me through the abundance of your love, and for the favors and graces you have granted me. You are truly my Good Shepherd, the Healer of my spirit and the Light that guides my path. At the hour of my death be with me, until that time when I join the saints in heaven to praise you forever. Amen.

Act of Consecration

I, [*your name*], give and consecrate to the Sacred Heart of our Lord Jesus Christ my person and my life, my actions, pains, and sufferings, wishing only to ever honor, love, and glorify that Sacred Heart.

It is my will to be entirely his, and to do everything for his love, renouncing with my whole heart whatever might displease him.

I take you then, O Sacred Heart, to be the sole object of my love, the protector of my life, the pledge of my salvation, the remedy of my frailty and inconstancy, the repairer of my sins, and my secure refuge in the hour of death.

O heart of goodness, be my justification before God your Father, and deliver me from punishment for my sins. O heart of love, I place all my confidence in you. While I fear all things from my weakness, I hope all things from your goodness.

Free me from whatever may offend you, and engrave yourself so deeply upon my heart that it will be impossible for me ever to forget you or be separated from you.

I ask you, by all your goodness, that my name may be written in you, since I desire that all my happiness and glory should consist in living and dying in service to you. Amen.

Saint Margaret Mary

Litany of the Sacred Heart of Jesus

Lord, have mercy on us.
Christ, have mercy on us.
Lord, have mercy on us.
God, our Father in heaven, *have mercy on us.*

God the Son, Redeemer
of the world, *have mercy on us.*

God the Holy Spirit, *have mercy on us.*

Holy Trinity, one God, *have mercy on us.*

Heart of Jesus, Son of the
Eternal Father, *have mercy on us.*

Heart of Jesus, formed by the
Holy Spirit in the womb
of the Virgin Mother, *have mercy on us.*

Heart of Jesus, one with
the eternal Word, *have mercy on us.*

Heart of Jesus, infinite in majesty, *have mercy on us.*

Heart of Jesus, holy temple
of God, *have mercy on us.*

Heart of Jesus, tabernacle of
the Most High, *have mercy on us.*

Heart of Jesus, house of God
and gate of heaven, *have mercy on us.*

Heart of Jesus, aflame with
love for us, *have mercy on us.*

Heart of Jesus, source of
justice and love, *have mercy on us.*

Heart of Jesus, full of
goodness and love, *have mercy on us.*

Heart of Jesus, wellspring
of all virtue, *have mercy on us.*

Heart of Jesus, worthy of
all praise, *have mercy on us.*

Heart of Jesus, king and center
of all hearts, *have mercy on us.*

Heart of Jesus, treasury of all
wisdom and knowledge, *have mercy on us.*

Heart of Jesus, in whom dwells
the fullness of divinity, *have mercy on us.*

Heart of Jesus, in whom the
Father is well pleased, *have mercy on us.*

Heart of Jesus, from whose
fullness we have all received, *have mercy on us.*

Heart of Jesus, desire of the
everlasting hills, *have mercy on us.*

Heart of Jesus, patient and
merciful, *have mercy on us.*

Heart of Jesus, generous to all
who turn to you,   *have mercy on us.*

Heart of Jesus, fountain of life
and holiness,   *have mercy on us.*

Heart of Jesus, atonement
for our sins,   *have mercy on us.*

Heart of Jesus, weighed down
with insult,   *have mercy on us.*

Heart of Jesus, bruised for
our offenses,   *have mercy on us.*

Heart of Jesus, obedient
even unto death,   *have mercy on us.*

Heart of Jesus, pierced
by a lance,   *have mercy on us.*

Heart of Jesus, source of all
consolation,   *have mercy on us.*

Heart of Jesus, our life
and resurrection,   *have mercy on us.*

Heart of Jesus, our peace
and reconciliation,   *have mercy on us.*

Heart of Jesus, victim for
our sins,   *have mercy on us.*

Heart of Jesus, salvation of all
who trust in you,   *have mercy on us.*

Heart of Jesus, hope of all
who die in you, *have mercy on us.*

Heart of Jesus, delight of
all the saints, *have mercy on us.*

Lamb of God, you take away the sins of the world,
spare us, O Lord.

Lamb of God, you take away the sins of the world,
graciously hear us, O Lord.

Lamb of God, you take away the sins of the world,
have mercy on us.

℣. Jesus, gentle and humble of heart,
℟. touch our hearts and make them like your
own.

Let us pray.

Father in heaven, we praise and thank you for the gifts of love we have received from the heart of your Son, Jesus. Teach us to see Christ in those whose lives we touch and to show our grateful love through service to our brothers and sisters. We ask this through Christ our Lord. Amen.

*Approved for use throughout
the universal Church by Leo XIII in 1899*

Devotions to the Infant of Prague

A Short Novena

Divine Infant Jesus of Prague, you who lovingly said, "Ask, and it shall be given you; seek, and you shall find; knock, and it shall be opened to you," through the intercession of Mary, your most holy Mother, I ask you for this grace [*mention your petition*].

Divine Infant Jesus of Prague, you who compassionately taught, "If you can believe, all things are possible to the one who believes," increase my weak faith, and through the intercession of Mary, your most holy Mother, grant my request [*mention your petition*].

Divine Infant Jesus of Prague, you who said to the Apostles, "If you have faith even like a mustard seed, you will say to this mulberry tree, 'Be uprooted and be planted in the sea,' and it will obey you," hear my prayer. Through the intercession of Mary, your most holy Mother, I am confident that you will answer my prayer [*mention your petition*].

For a Special Intention

Divine Infant Jesus, with confident hope in your unfailing protection and faithful providence I seek your help in my time of need, through the intercession of Mary, your Mother [*mention your request*].

I am sorry for my sins. I resolve to sin no more and to avoid the occasions of sin, so that I may never offend you again. I want to do my utmost to accept the daily hardships of life and to love my neighbor as myself, so as to serve you more faithfully until the day I can join the saints and angels in heaven to praise you forever. Amen.

From a prayer by Rev. Cyril of the Mother of God,
the first to promote devotion to the Infant of Prague

Prayer for Children

Divine Infant, we ask you to bless all the children of the world. Grant them your Spirit's gifts of wisdom and prudence, that they may follow the path of goodness and integrity. Give them health of mind

and body and the spiritual strength to overcome temptation.

Watch over children who are missing and young runaways; keep them free from harm and return them quickly to their loved ones. Safeguard those who suffer hunger, abuse, and exploitation; preserve their well-being and innocence. Grant that children in foster care and those in need of adoption find loving and warm homes that offer security and stability.

Lord Jesus, send your angels to protect and guide all children along the path of life, until the day they join you and the saints in heaven forever. Amen.

Devotions to the Divine Mercy

The Chaplet of Divine Mercy

(A five-decade rosary can be used)

In this prayer we offer the body and blood, soul and divinity of Jesus Christ to God the Father, and we unite ourselves with his sacrifice offered on the cross for the salvation of the world. We ask for mercy for ourselves and for the whole world, that is, all people living on earth as well as the souls in purgatory.

Begin with an Our Father (p. 5), a Hail Mary (p. 5) and the Apostles' Creed (p. 16).

On the large bead before each decade, pray:

Eternal Father, I offer you the body and blood, soul and divinity of your dearly beloved Son, our Lord Jesus Christ, in atonement for our sins and those of the whole world.

On the ten small beads of each decade, pray:

For the sake of his sorrowful passion, have mercy on us and on the whole world.

After the five decades, conclude with:

Holy God, Holy Mighty One, Holy Immortal One, have mercy on us and on the whole world *(three times)*.

Prayers from Saint Faustina's Diary

Invocations of Trust

O my God, my only hope, I have placed all my trust in you, and I know I shall not be disappointed (317).

I know the full power of your mercy, and I trust that you will give me everything your weak child needs (898).

O Jesus, concealed in the Blessed Sacrament of the Altar, my only love and mercy, I commend to you all the needs of my body and soul. You can help me, because you are mercy itself. In you lies all my hope (1751).

Prayer of Trust

I fly to your mercy, compassionate God, who alone are good. Although my misery is great and my offenses are many, I trust in your mercy because you are the God of mercy; and, from time immemorial, it has never been heard of, nor do heaven or earth remember, that a soul trusting in your mercy has been disappointed.

O God of compassion, you alone can justify me, and you will never reject me when I, contrite, approach your merciful heart, where no one has ever been refused, even if he were the greatest sinner (1730).

In Thanksgiving

O Jesus, eternal God, thank you for your countless graces and blessings. Let every beat of my heart be a new hymn of thanksgiving to you, O God. Let every drop of my blood circulate for you, Lord. My soul is one hymn in adoration of your mercy. I love you, God, for yourself alone (1794).

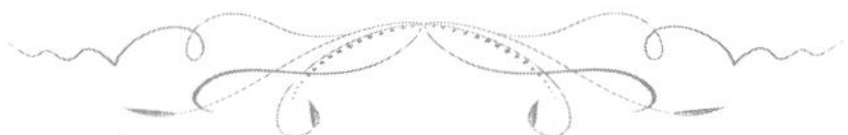

Devotion to the Precious Blood

Litany of the Precious Blood

Lord, have mercy.	*Lord, have mercy.*
Christ, have mercy.	*Christ, have mercy.*
Lord, have mercy.	*Lord, have mercy.*
God our Father in heaven,	*have mercy on us.*
God the Son, Redeemer of the world,	*have mercy on us.*
God the Holy Spirit,	*have mercy on us.*
Holy Trinity, one God,	*have mercy on us.*
Blood of Christ, only-begotten Son of the eternal Father,	*save us.*
Blood of Christ, incarnate Word of God,	*save us.*
Blood of Christ, of the new and eternal covenant,	*save us.*

Blood of Christ, spilled upon
   the earth in agony, *save us.*

Blood of Christ, shed freely in
   the scourging, *save us.*

Blood of Christ, streaming forth
   from the crown of thorns, *save us.*

Blood of Christ, poured out on the cross, *save us.*

Blood of Christ, price of our redemption, *save us.*

Blood of Christ, offering forgiveness
   and pardon for sin, *save us.*

Blood of Christ, eucharistic refreshment
   of souls, *save us.*

Blood of Christ, river of mercy, *save us.*

Blood of Christ, victor over evil, *save us.*

Blood of Christ, strength of martyrs, *save us.*

Blood of Christ, fortitude of the saints, *save us.*

Blood of Christ, sustenance of virgins, *save us.*

Blood of Christ, help of those in peril, *save us.*

Blood of Christ, relief of the burdened, *save us.*

Blood of Christ, solace in sorrow, *save us.*

Blood of Christ, hope of the repentant, *save us.*

Blood of Christ, consolation of the dying, *save us.*

Blood of Christ, peace and comfort
for hearts,   *save us.*

Blood of Christ, pledge of eternal life,   *save us.*

Blood of Christ, hope of glory,   *save us.*

Blood of Christ, most worthy of all honor,   *save us.*

Lamb of God, you take away the sins of the world,
have mercy on us.

Lamb of God, you take away the sins of the world,
have mercy on us.

Lamb of God, you take away the sins of the world,
have mercy on us.

℣. You redeemed us by your blood, O Lord.
℟. And made us a kingdom to serve our God.

Let us pray.

Almighty and eternal God, you gave your Son to us to be our Redeemer. Grant that his saving blood be a safeguard against every evil, so that we may rejoice in its fruits forever in heaven. Through the same Christ our Lord. Amen.

Approved by Saint John XXIII (1881–1963)
for the universal Church

Devotion to the Holy Name of Jesus

Litany of the Holy Name of Jesus

Lord, have mercy.

Christ, have mercy.

Lord, have mercy.

Jesus, hear us.

Jesus, graciously hear us.

God the Father of heaven, *have mercy on us.*

God the Son, Redeemer of the world, *have mercy on us.*

God the Holy Spirit, *have mercy on us.*

Holy Trinity, one God, *have mercy on us.*

Jesus, Son of the living God, *have mercy on us.*

Jesus, splendor of the Father, *have mercy on us.*

Jesus, brightness of eternal light, *have mercy on us.*

Jesus, king of glory,   *have mercy on us.*

Jesus, sun of justice,   *have mercy on us.*

Jesus, Son of the Virgin Mary,   *have mercy on us.*

Jesus, most amiable,   *have mercy on us.*

Jesus, most admirable,   *have mercy on us.*

Jesus, the mighty God,   *have mercy on us.*

Jesus, father of the world to come,   *have mercy on us.*

Jesus, wonderful counselor,   *have mercy on us.*

Jesus, most powerful,   *have mercy on us.*

Jesus, most patient,   *have mercy on us.*

Jesus, most obedient,   *have mercy on us.*

Jesus, meek and humble of heart,   *have mercy on us.*

Jesus, lover of chastity,   *have mercy on us.*

Jesus, lover of us all,   *have mercy on us.*

Jesus, God of peace,   *have mercy on us.*

Jesus, author of life,   *have mercy on us.*

Jesus, example of virtue,   *have mercy on us.*

Jesus, ardent lover of souls,   *have mercy on us.*

Jesus, our God,   *have mercy on us.*

Jesus, our refuge,   *have mercy on us.*

Jesus, father of the poor,   *have mercy on us.*

Jesus, treasure of the faithful,   *have mercy on us.*

Jesus, Good Shepherd, *have mercy on us.*

Jesus, true light, *have mercy on us.*

Jesus, eternal wisdom, *have mercy on us.*

Jesus, infinite goodness, *have mercy on us.*

Jesus, our way and our life, *have mercy on us.*

Jesus, joy of the angels, *have mercy on us.*

Jesus, king of the patriarchs, *have mercy on us.*

Jesus, master of the apostles, *have mercy on us.*

Jesus, teacher of the evangelists, *have mercy on us.*

Jesus, strength of martyrs, *have mercy on us.*

Jesus, light of confessors, *have mercy on us.*

Jesus, purity of virgins, *have mercy on us.*

Jesus, crown of all saints, *have mercy on us.*

Be merciful, *spare us, O Jesus.*

Be merciful, *graciously hear us, O Jesus.*

From every evil, *deliver us, O Jesus.*

From all sin, *deliver us, O Jesus.*

From your anger, *deliver us, O Jesus.*

From the snares of the devil, *deliver us, O Jesus.*

From the spirit of impurity, *deliver us, O Jesus.*

From everlasting death, *deliver us, O Jesus.*

From neglect of your
inspirations, *deliver us, O Jesus.*

By the mystery of your incarnation,	*deliver us, O Jesus.*
By your birth,	*deliver us, O Jesus.*
By your infancy,	*deliver us, O Jesus.*
By your life and ministry,	*deliver us, O Jesus.*
By your agony and abandonment,	*deliver us, O Jesus.*
By your sufferings and crucifixion,	*deliver us, O Jesus.*
By your death and burial,	*deliver us, O Jesus.*
By your resurrection from the dead,	*deliver us, O Jesus.*
By your ascension into heaven,	*deliver us, O Jesus.*
By your gift of the Holy Eucharist,	*deliver us, O Jesus.*
By your joy and glory,	*deliver us, O Jesus.*

Lamb of God, who take away the sins of the world,
spare us, O Jesus.

Lamb of God, who take away the sins of the world,
graciously hear us, O Jesus.

Lamb of God, who take away the sins of the world,
have mercy on us, O Jesus.

℣. Jesus, hear us.

℟. Jesus, graciously hear us.

Let us pray.

O Lord Jesus Christ, you have said, "Ask and you shall receive; seek, and you shall find; knock, and it shall be opened to you"; mercifully grant us the grace of your divine love and a reverence for your holy name, that we may love you with all our hearts and in all our words and actions, and never cease to praise you, who live and reign forever and ever. Amen.

Approved by Leo XIII (1810–1903)
for the universal Church

EUCHARISTIC DEVOTIONS

Prayer of Adoration

Jesus, today's adoration is the meeting of my soul
    and all of my being with you.
I am the creature meeting the Creator;
the disciple before the Divine Master;
the patient with the Doctor of souls;
the poor one appealing to the Rich One;
the thirsty one drinking at the Font;
the weak before the Almighty;
the tempted seeking a sure Refuge;
the blind person searching for the Light;
the friend who goes to the True Friend;
the lost sheep sought by the Divine Shepherd;
the wayward heart who finds the Way;
the unenlightened one who finds Wisdom;
the bride who find the Spouse of the soul;

the "nothing" who finds the All;
the afflicted who finds the Consoler;
the seeker who finds life's meaning.

Blessed James Alberione

Credo, Adoro, Amo
(I Believe, I Adore, I Love)

Credo: I believe, Lord, that you are truly, substantially present in the Blessed Sacrament: the same God incarnate who became like us in all things, except sin, and redeemed us by your supreme act of love on Calvary.

Credo: I believe. What else could I do? You have the words of eternal life: "Take this, all of you, and eat it; this is my body. Take this, all of you, and drink from it; this is the cup of my blood, the blood of the new and everlasting covenant. It will be shed for you and for all so that sins may be forgiven."

Credo: I believe, Lord, increase my faith.

Adoro: I adore you, Lord, the Alpha and the Omega, the Beginning and the End of my life, without whose divine Providence I could not draw a breath or move a limb.

All that I am, all that I have, I owe to you. Without you I am nothing and can do nothing. You are my God and my all. Help me to be totally dedicated to you.

I offer myself as your hands and feet to run errands of charity in your name. Yes, I give myself to you as a living tool in your hands—as your servant, if need be.

Adoro: I adore you, O Lord, with every fiber of my being.

Amo: I love you, O Lord, with my whole heart and soul, not for what you will give me but for what you are—Infinite Love. If I cannot love you with the immaculate love of your Blessed Mother, give me the grace to love you with the penitent heart of a Magdalene. If I cannot love you with the angelic love of a Saint John, give me the grace to love you with the penitent heart of a Peter.

Amo: I love you, O Lord, with my whole heart and soul.

Prayer Before the Blessed Sacrament

Jesus, my Lord and my God, Creator and Ruler of the universe, I lovingly adore you, hidden so

humbly beneath the appearances of the fragile host. I am in awe to reflect that as I kneel before the Blessed Sacrament, I am not venerating a relic but worshiping the infinite God. I rejoice that the Blessed Sacrament is not merely a holy thing but a living Person—the same Christ who died on Calvary for each and every one of us, but who loved us so much that he wanted to remain with us forever.

Dear sacramental Savior, when you rose gloriously from the tomb you showed your infinite power, but when you remain silently in the tabernacle you show your infinite love.

Like the Wise Men who worshiped you in Bethlehem under a dazzling star, I adore you under the soft glow of the sanctuary lamp during this Eucharistic hour. I cannot bring you the gifts of the Magi, but I lay at your feet my heart and soul, my very life.

Bless our Holy Father, the Pope, and the Church throughout the world. Bless those who suffer persecution for your sake, and those who preach your Gospel in distant lands. Bless our priests, our religious sisters and brothers, and increase their numbers. Bless my family and my dear departed loved ones, the sick and the homebound, those who have wandered from your fold and those who are searching for the truth.

You were my First Communion; be also the Viaticum of my old age. But in between, may you ever be my daily Bread, so that Holy Communion here on earth may be for me a sweet foretaste of an eternal union with you in heaven. Amen.

Anima Christi
(Soul of Christ)

Soul of Christ, sanctify me.
Body of Christ, save me.
Blood of Christ, cleanse me.
Water from the side of Christ, wash me.
Passion of Christ, strengthen me.
Good Jesus, hear me.
Within your wounds hide me.
Never let me be parted from you.
From the evil one protect me.
In the hour of my death, call me
and bid me come to you,
that with your saints I may praise you
forever and ever. Amen.

Thanksgiving for the Gift of the Eucharist

Jesus, Divine Master, I thank and praise you for the great gift of the Holy Eucharist. Your love makes you dwell in the holy tabernacle, renew your passion in the Mass, and give yourself as our spiritual food in Holy Communion. Grant that I may better know you, O hidden God, and draw abundant waters from the font of your heart. Give me the privilege and grace to visit you often in this sacrament, to better understand and devoutly participate in the Mass, and to receive you often in Holy Communion, with faith and love. Amen.

Blessed James Alberione

For Faith in the Real Presence

I come to you, Lord, like the Apostles, to pray, "Increase my faith." Give me a strong and lively faith that you are really present in the Eucharist; an active faith that will direct my life.

Give me the remarkable faith of the Centurion, which drew forth such praise from you. Give me the faith of the Beloved Disciple to recognize you and exclaim, "It is the Lord!" Give me the faith of Peter

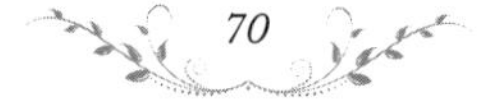

to confess, "You are the Christ, Son of the living God!" Give me the faith of Mary Magdalene to bow down at your feet and cry out, "Rabboni! Master!"

Give me the faith of all the saints to whom the Eucharist was heaven begun here on earth. Each time I receive the Eucharist and each time I make a visit to the Blessed Sacrament, increase my faith and love, my humility and reverence, and my trust that all good things will come to me.

My Lord and my God, increase my faith!

Act of Trust in Jesus' Promises

Jesus, I believe you are the Word who became flesh and lived among us, offering us grace and truth.

Jesus, I believe you are the Lamb of God who takes away our sins.

Jesus, I believe you are the Master who invites us to discipleship, growth, and an ever greater love.

Jesus, I believe you are God's beloved Son, sent into the world to save us.

Jesus, I believe you are Living Water, who quenches our thirst for meaning, love, peace, and truth, offering us abundant life.

Jesus, I believe you are the Bread of Life, broken
and given for the life of the world.
Jesus, I believe you are the Light of the world,
who frees us from darkness and answers the
deepest questions of our hearts.
Jesus, I believe you are the Good Shepherd, who
laid down his life for us and keeps us safe,
and who calls us to shepherd others.
Jesus, I believe you are the Resurrection, promis-
ing eternal life to all who believe in you.
Jesus, I believe you are the Master who became
the servant of all.
Jesus, I believe you are the living and true Vine
who promises plentiful fruit and life.
Jesus, I believe you are the Way, the Truth, and
the Life of the world, inviting us to be transformed in you.

Suggested Method for
an Hour of Adoration

At the center of Eucharistic devotion is Jesus, our Way, Truth, and Life. Jesus not only proclaims the truth but is himself our *Truth*, because in him we discover the loving face of God. Jesus is the *Way* to the Father not just by his example but also because he walks with us on our daily journey. As our *Life*, Jesus saves us from sin and invites us to experience the fullness of life in him. Our deepening relationship with Jesus, Way, Truth, and Life, transforms us and our relationships: we become more loving and committed to advancing the kingdom of God here on earth.

The following method for making an hour of adoration is inspired by the Pauline spirituality of Blessed James Alberione, Founder of the Pauline Family. He wrote: "The hour of adoration is our time each day for a private 'audience' with Jesus; we meet with him and enter into intimate conversation with him."

The Pauline hour of adoration has three parts or "moments," based on Jesus' definition of himself as Way, Truth, and Life.

First Moment:
Adoring Jesus Truth

As you prepare to read the Word of God during this moment, allow yourself to enter into the school of Jesus Master as his disciple. Welcome the light of his truth; savor it and let it shape your mind and attitudes. The following steps are helpful to follow:

- Begin with a hymn or a prayer of adoration.
- Ask for the light of the Holy Spirit to open your mind and heart to his word.
- Select and read a passage from Scripture that corresponds to a specific theme or a particular need you are bringing to prayer.
- Listen with your heart to understand how Jesus is speaking to you through his word.
- Speak to Jesus about how this reading touches your life, and then conclude with a personal act of faith.

Suggested Scripture passages:

Matthew 5:13–16	Salt and Light
Matthew 6:25–34	Trust in God
Matthew 7:7–11	The Power of Prayer

Mark 4:35–41	The Storm on the Lake (Faith)
Mark 10:46–52	Blind Bartimeus (Faith)
Luke 9:57–62	The Cost of Discipleship
Luke 11:1–13	On Prayer
John 6:49–71	The Bread of Life
John 10:1–21	The Good Shepherd

Second Moment:
Following Jesus Way

In the light of your Scripture reading, contemplate the holiness of Jesus, our Way and Model, in order to look more closely at your relationship with him. The examination of conscience is the moment in which we enter into the heart of Jesus and discover his wisdom, imitate his virtues, conform ourselves to him, and allow him to dwell within us.

Recall those times in which you have experienced the action of God in your life, and then pray an act of thanksgiving for all the graces and blessings you have received.

Invite the Holy Spirit to be present as you take a few moments to examine your thoughts, actions,

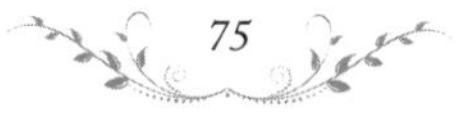

attitudes, and motivations. Speak to the Lord especially about what is in your heart that is sinful, then resolve to follow Jesus more faithfully.

Pray an act of sorrow and allow the healing work of grace to penetrate your soul.

Suggested prayers to use during this moment:

Prayer of Thanksgiving: Canticle of Mary,
   p. 117 (Magnificat, p. 281 in Latin)
Psalms of Thanksgiving: 113, 146, 148, 149
Act of Contrition, p. 9, or Psalm 51

THIRD MOMENT:
SHARING JESUS' LIFE

Open your heart to Jesus; allow his life-nourishing grace to fill your soul and transform your life, so that you can bring his love and peace to others.

Speak to Jesus about your deepest desires for yourself and for your loved ones.

Place your needs, those of the Church, and those of the world before our loving God.

Pray spontaneously or select a psalm to pray. You may also choose to pray the Liturgy of the Hours, the Rosary, the Stations of the Cross, or other favorite prayers.

Conclude your time of adoration by offering to the Lord one way in which you can be his presence in the world.

Suggested Prayers:

The Rosary, p. 83

The Way of the Cross, p. 254

Prayers for Eucharistic Adoration, p. 65

PRAYERS TO OUR LADY

THE HOLY ROSARY

The Rosary is a contemplative Gospel prayer. With the calm, rhythmic recitation of vocal prayers, we focus our attention inwardly on the living mysteries of the life, death, and resurrection of Jesus Christ. As we ponder these mysteries, we are doing what Mary herself did. With Mary, we recall the mysteries of Jesus' life and with her we "learn Christ." We learn to live a life of faith and become a faith-filled disciple of the Lord.

The Rosary, in the prayer-form familiar to us today, developed through the centuries. The term "rosary" derives from the Latin "rosarium," meaning "rose garden," which in earliest tradition was linked to a passage in the Hebrew Scriptures' Song of Songs (2:1). The beautiful woman who dwells in the garden was associated with the Virgin Mary, "rose of Sharon and lily of the valley." By the fourteenth century, however, the term "rosarium" had come to mean a collection of devotional texts.

During the Middle Ages, when most people were illiterate, various ways were devised for them to participate in the recitation of the 150 psalms used in the Church's Divine Office. At first, many would recite the Our Father 150 times; later, the first part of the Hail Mary was recited. Thus was born "Our Lady's Psalter." The second part of the Hail Mary (Holy Mary, Mother of God . . .) appeared in the Roman Breviary in 1568. Up until that time various phrases referring to the lives of Jesus and Mary were interposed after the name Jesus. As the centuries passed, these interjections evolved into the "mysteries" of the Rosary.

Like most of the elements of the Rosary, the use of the term "rosary" as a form of prayer as well as the actual physical object took place gradually. The use of beads is not a practice common to Christians only. A string of beads as a tool to count a number of prayers is known in Buddhism, Hinduism, and Islam. The early Desert Fathers and Mothers used ropes with knots or simple pebbles to count the number of prayers or psalms they recited each day. Then as today the knots, pebbles, or beads were tangible symbols of an inner attitude of prayer and meditation.

The practice of praying the Rosary grew among the faithful when the liturgical feast was established in 1573 by Saint Pius V, and as the Dominican Order popularized its recitation, preaching throughout Europe the spiritual benefits gained from praying the Rosary. In subsequent years Rosary Confraternities were formed throughout the world; saints and popes through the centuries have promoted and practiced this devotion. The Rosary is a prayer easily adapted to diverse circumstances, needs, and groups: families, prayer groups, Holy Hours, wakes, parish gatherings. The Rosary is an invitation, a path and help to deepen one's prayer life in the company of Mary.

HOW TO PRAY THE ROSARY

Begin the Rosary by making the Sign of the Cross (p. 2); then, while holding the crucifix, pray the Apostles' Creed (p. 16). On the beads of the small chain pray one Our Father (p. 5), three Hail Marys (p. 5), and one Glory to the Father (p. 5). Next, announce the mystery and pray one Our Father, ten Hail Marys, and a Glory to the Father. This completes one decade. All the other decades are prayed in the same manner, while pondering the

mystery for each decade. Pray the Hail, Holy Queen
(p. 11) at the end and, if you wish, the Litany of
Loreto (p. 94).

JOYFUL MYSTERIES

Usually prayed on Mondays and Saturdays

1. The Annunciation of the Angel to Mary

"The Angel Gabriel was sent from God . . . to a
virgin who was betrothed to a man . . . named Joseph,
and the virgin's name was Mary. And when he came
into her presence he said, 'Hail, full of grace, the
Lord is with you!' She was perplexed by these words
and wondered what sort of greeting this could be.

"Mary said, 'Behold the handmaid of the Lord;
let it be done to me according to your word'" (Lk
1:26–29, 38).

Grace to ask: To know and embrace God's will in
my life.

Invocation: Jesus, meek and humble, live in me.

2. Mary Visits Her Cousin Elizabeth

"And when she entered the house of Zechariah
she greeted Elizabeth. And it happened when

Elizabeth heard Mary's greeting the baby leapt in her womb, Elizabeth was filled with the Holy Spirit, and she exclaimed with a loud cry, 'Blessed are you among women, and blessed is the fruit of your womb!'" (Lk 1:40–42)

> *Grace to ask:* To be attentive to the needs of those around me.
>
> *Invocation:* Jesus most loving, live in me.

3. The Birth of Jesus at Bethlehem

"Now it happened that in those days a decree went out from Caesar Augustus that all the world should be registered. . . . Since Joseph was of the house and family of David, he went up from Nazareth in Galilee to Bethlehem of Judea, the city of David to be registered with Mary, who was betrothed to him and who was pregnant. It happened that while they were there the day came for her to give birth. She gave birth to her firstborn son, wrapped him in swaddling clothes, and laid him in a manger, because there was no room for them in the inn" (Lk 2:1, 4–7).

> *Grace to ask:* To be attentive to the needs of the poor and homeless.
>
> *Invocation:* Jesus, poor and selfless, live in me.

4. The Presentation of Jesus in the Temple

"They took the child up to Jerusalem to present him to the Lord. . . . And when the parents brought the child Jesus in [to the Temple] to do for him what was in accordance with the custom of the Torah, [Simeon] took him in his arms and blessed God, saying, 'Now you send your servant away in peace, O Master, according to your word, because my eyes have seen your salvation. . . .' His father and mother were amazed at what was said about Jesus. And Simeon blessed them and said to his mother, Mary, 'Behold, he is destined to bring about the fall and rise of many in Israel'" (Lk 2:22–34).

> *Grace to ask:* To open my heart to the wisdom of God.
>
> *Invocation:* Lord, help me to grow in spiritual awareness.

5. The Finding of Jesus in the Temple

"And when he was twelve years old they went up to Jerusalem in accordance with the custom of the feast, and . . . while they were returning, the child Jesus remained in Jerusalem, but his parents did not know. . . . And it happened that after three days they found him in the Temple, seated in the midst of the

teachers, both listening to them and asking them questions, and all those listening to him were amazed at his intelligence and his answers" (Lk 2:42–48).

Grace to ask: To carry out difficult tasks with patience.

Invocation: Jesus, loving and patient, live in me.

LUMINOUS MYSTERIES

Usually prayed on Thursdays

1. John Baptizes Jesus in the Jordan

"At that time Jesus came from Galilee to be baptized by John at the Jordan. John tried to prevent him and said, 'I need to be baptized by you, and you are coming to me?' But in answer Jesus said to him, 'Let it be, for now—it is fitting for us to fulfill all God's will in this way.' Then he let him. After he was baptized Jesus at once came up from the water, and, behold, the heavens were opened and he saw the Spirit of God descending upon him like a dove. And, behold, a voice from heaven said, 'This is my beloved Son in whom I am well pleased!'" (Mt 3:13–17)

Grace to ask: To live my baptismal promises.

Invocation: Holy Spirit, increase my hope.

2. Jesus Reveals His Glory at the Wedding at Cana

"On the third day there was a wedding in Cana of Galilee, and Jesus' mother was there. Now Jesus and his disciples had also been invited to the wedding, and when the wine ran out Jesus' mother said to him, 'They have no wine.' Jesus replied, 'What do you want from me, woman? My hour has not come yet.' His mother said to the servants, 'Do whatever he tells you.' . . .

"When the head steward tasted the water which had become wine . . . [he said], '. . . you have kept the good wine till now!' Jesus did this, the first of his signs, at Cana in Galilee and revealed his glory, and his disciples believed in him" (Jn 2:1–10, 11–12).

Grace to ask: To be attentive to the signs of God working in my life.

Invocation: Holy Spirit, increase my faith.

3. Jesus Proclaims the Kingdom of God and Calls Us to Conversion

"After John was arrested, Jesus came into Galilee proclaiming the good news of God and saying, 'The appointed time has come and the Kingdom of God

is as hand; repent and believe in the good news!'"
(Mk 1:14–15)

> *Grace to ask:* For authenticity of life.
> *Invocation:* Holy Spirit, grant that I may always
> be a true disciple of Jesus.

4. The Transfiguration of Jesus

"Jesus took Peter and James and John along and led them up a high mountain all alone. He was transformed in front of them and his clothes became an utterly glistening white, so white that no one on earth could bleach them that way.

"Then a cloud arose overshadowing them, and a voice from the cloud said, 'This is my beloved Son, hear him!' And suddenly as they looked around they no longer saw anyone but Jesus alone with them" (Mk 9:2–3, 7).

> *Grace to ask:* That my actions will always reflect
> the light of Christ.
> *Invocation:* Holy Spirit, grant that the light of
> the Gospel may reach the darkest corners
> of the world.

5. Jesus Gives Us the Eucharist

"And while they were eating he took bread, blessed it, broke it, gave it to them and said, 'Take it; this is my body.' And taking the cup, he blessed it and gave it to them and they all drank from it. Then he said to them, 'This is my blood of the covenant, which will be poured out for many. Amen, I say to you, I will not drink again of the fruit of the vine until that day when I drink it new in the Kingdom of God'" (Mk 14:22–25).

Grace to ask: To be a Christ-bearer for the world.
Invocation: Holy Spirit, show me how I can
serve others.

Sorrowful Mysteries

Usually prayed on Tuesdays and Fridays

1. Jesus Prays in the Garden of Gethsemane

"When they came to a place named Gethsemane he said to his disciples, 'Sit here while I pray' . . .

"Then he went ahead a little, fell on the ground, and prayed that, if it were possible, this moment might pass away from him, and he said, 'Abba, Father, all things are possible for you; take this cup from me,

but not what I wish, but what you do'" (Mk 14:32, 35–36).

Grace to ask: For the gift of a prayerful heart.
Invocation: Heavenly Father, not my will but yours be done.

2. Jesus Is Scourged

"So Pilate . . . to satisfy the crowd, released Barabbas to them, and after having Jesus scourged he handed him over to be crucified" (Mk 15:15).

Grace to ask: For the gift of a forgiving heart.
Invocation: Heavenly Father, I ask pardon of all whom I have injured.

3. Jesus Is Crowned with Thorns

"They stripped him and put a scarlet robe on him, and after weaving a crown of thorns they put it on his head and placed a reed in his right hand, then they knelt before him and mocked him, saying, 'Hail, King of the Jews!' And after spitting on him they took the reed and beat him over the head" (Mt 27:28–30).

Grace to ask: For freedom from self-gratification.
Invocation: Heavenly Father, grant me a spirit of self-sacrifice.

4. Jesus Carries the Cross to Calvary

"And carrying the cross himself he went out to what was called 'the Place of the Skull,' in Hebrew, Golgotha, where they crucified him and with him two others, on either side, while Jesus was in the middle" (Jn 19:17–18).

> *Grace to ask:* To comprehend the value of suffering.
>
> *Invocation:* Heavenly Father, comfort all those who suffer.

5. Jesus Is Crucified

"Now standing by Jesus' cross were his mother and his mother's sister, Mary the wife of Clopas, and Mary Magdalen. When Jesus saw his mother and the disciple he loved standing by he said to his mother, 'Woman, here is your son.' Then he said to the disciple, 'Here is your mother.' And from that hour the disciple took her into his home" (Jn 19:25–27).

> *Grace to ask:* For deliverance from a sudden death.
>
> *Invocation:* Heavenly Father, I believe in the resurrection of the body and life everlasting.

Glorious Mysteries

Usually prayed on Wednesdays and Sundays

1. Jesus Rises from the Dead

"Now after the Sabbath, as it began to dawn on the first day of the week, Mary Magdalen and the other Mary came to see the sepulcher. And, behold, there was a powerful earthquake; an angel of the Lord came down from Heaven, came up to the stone, rolled it away and sat upon it. . . . The angel said to the women, 'Don't be afraid—I know you are looking for Jesus, who was crucified. He isn't here—he is risen, just like he said'" (Mt 28:1–2, 5–6).

Grace to ask: For an increase in the virtue of hope.
Invocation: Lord, I trust in your promise of
    eternal life.

2. Jesus Ascends into Heaven

"After he said these things he was taken up while they watched, and a cloud took him out of their sight. While they were gazing up at the sky as he departed, behold, two men in white garments stood beside them and said, 'Men of Galilee, why are you standing here looking up at the sky? This Jesus who has been taken from you up to Heaven will return in

the same way you saw him going up to Heaven'"
(Acts 1:9–11).

> *Grace to ask:* To be a messenger of the Gospel to
> all whom I meet.
>
> *Invocation:* Lord, may your kingdom come.

3. The Holy Spirit Descends on the Apostles

"Now when the day of Pentecost arrived they
were all together in one place. Suddenly a sound like
a violent rushing wind came from the sky and filled
the whole house where they were staying. Tongues as
if of fire appeared to them, parting and coming to
rest on each of them, and they were all filled with the
Holy Spirit and began to speak in different tongues
according to how the Spirit inspired them to speak"
(Acts 2:1–4).

> *Grace to ask:* For an outpouring of the gifts of the
> Holy Spirit.
>
> *Invocation:* Lord, preserve unity among all
> Christians.

4. Mary Is Assumed into Heaven

"And if I go and prepare a place for you,
I will come again and take you to myself,
So that where I am, you too may be" (Jn 14:3).

Grace to ask: For the gift of spiritual joy.

Invocation: Lord, grant that all who will die this
day may have eternal life with you.

5. Mary Is Crowned Queen of Heaven and Earth

"Then a great sign was seen in the sky—a woman
clothed with the sun, with the moon beneath her feet
and a crown of twelve stars on her head" (Rev 12:1).

Grace to ask: To respect the dignity of each and
every person.

Invocation: Lord, grant that all Christians may
be strong in their faith and selfless in their
love.

Litany of Loreto

Lord, have mercy on us.

Christ, have mercy on us

Lord, have mercy on us.

Christ, hear us.

Christ, graciously hear us.

God the Father of heaven, *have mercy on us.*

God the Son, Redeemer
of the world, *have mercy on us.*

God the Holy Spirit, *have mercy on us.*

Holy Trinity, one God,	*have mercy on us.*
Holy Mary,	*pray for us.*
Holy Mother of God,	*pray for us.*
Holy Virgin of virgins,	*pray for us.*
Mother of Christ,	*pray for us.*
Mother of Divine Grace,	*pray for us.*
Mother of hope,	*pray for us.*
Mother most pure,	*pray for us.*
Mother most chaste,	*pray for us.*
Mother inviolate,	*pray for us.*
Mother undefiled,	*pray for us.*
Mother most amiable,	*pray for us.*
Mother most admirable,	*pray for us.*
Mother of good counsel,	*pray for us.*
Mother of our Creator,	*pray for us.*
Mother of our Savior,	*pray for us.*
Mother of the Church,	*pray for us.*
Mother of mercy,	*pray for us.*
Virgin most prudent,	*pray for us.*
Virgin most venerable,	*pray for us.*
Virgin most renowned,	*pray for us.*
Virgin most powerful,	*pray for us.*
Virgin most merciful,	*pray for us.*

Virgin most faithful, *pray for us.*

Mirror of justice, *pray for us.*

Seat of wisdom, *pray for us.*

Cause of our joy, *pray for us.*

Spiritual vessel, *pray for us.*

Vessel of honor, *pray for us.*

Singular vessel of devotion, *pray for us.*

Mystical rose, *pray for us.*

Tower of David, *pray for us.*

Tower of ivory, *pray for us.*

House of gold, *pray for us.*

Ark of the covenant, *pray for us.*

Gate of Heaven, *pray for us.*

Morning star, *pray for us.*

Health of the sick, *pray for us.*

Refuge of sinners, *pray for us.*

Comfort of migrants, *pray for us.*

Comforter of the afflicted, *pray for us.*

Help of Christians, *pray for us.*

Queen of angels, *pray for us.*

Queen of patriarchs, *pray for us.*

Queen of prophets, *pray for us.*

Queen of apostles, *pray for us.*

Queen of martyrs,	*pray for us.*
Queen of confessors,	*pray for us.*
Queen of virgins,	*pray for us.*
Queen of all saints,	*pray for us.*
Queen conceived without original sin,	*pray for us.*
Queen assumed into Heaven,	*pray for us.*
Queen of the holy Rosary,	*pray for us.*
Queen of families,	*pray for us.*
Queen of peace,	*pray for us.*

Lamb of God, who takes away the sins of the world, *spare us, O Lord.*

Lamb of God, who takes away the sins of the world, *graciously spare us, O Lord.*

Lamb of God, who takes away the sins of the world, *have mercy on us.*

℣. Pray for us, O holy Mother of God.

℟. That we may be made worthy of the promises of Christ.

During Ordinary Time

Let us pray. O God, whose only-begotten Son, by his life, death, and resurrection, has purchased for us the rewards of eternal life, grant, we beseech you, that by meditating upon these mysteries of the most holy

Rosary of the Blessed Virgin Mary, we may imitate what they contain, and obtain what they promise. Through Christ our Lord. Amen.

During Advent

Let us pray. O God, you willed that, at the message of an angel, your Word should take flesh in the womb of the Blessed Virgin Mary; grant to your suppliant people that we who believe her to be truly the Mother of God may be helped by her intercession with you. Through the same Christ our Lord. Amen.

From Christmas to the Feast of the Purification

Let us pray. O God, by the fruitful virginity of Blessed Mary, you bestowed upon the human race the rewards of eternal salvation; grant, we beg you, that we may feel the power of her intercession, through whom we have been made worthy to receive the Author of life, our Lord Jesus Christ your Son, who lives and reigns with you forever and ever. Amen.

Let us pray. O God, who by the resurrection of your Son, our Lord Jesus Christ, granted joy to the whole world, grant, we beg you, that through the intercession of the Virgin Mary, his Mother, we may attain the joys of eternal life. Through the same Christ our Lord. Amen.

Saint Bernard's Prayer

Remember, O most gracious Virgin Mary, that never was it known that anyone who fled to your protection, implored your help, or sought your intercession was left unaided. Inspired with this confidence, I fly to you, O Virgin of virgins, my Mother. To you I come, before you I stand, sinful and sorrowful. O Mother of the Word Incarnate, despise not my petitions, but in your mercy hear and answer me. Amen.

Fatima Prayer

O my Jesus, forgive us our sins. Save us from the fires of hell. Lead all souls to heaven, especially those who have most need of your mercy.

Various Marian Prayers

Marian devotion has a long and esteemed history in the Church. Early Christians readily understood the natural connection between Mary and her Son; therefore, honoring the Mother of Jesus was a recognized way to pay tribute to Jesus Christ. From the very beginning of Christianity, devotion to Mary pointed to devotion to Jesus. The Church honors Mary because God honored her first by choosing her to be the Mother of his Son.

We pray to Mary because we believe that God has given her to us as a Mother who will always intercede for her children. We honor her for her fidelity to God. We ask for her intercession for our needs and that we may know and honor her Son, Jesus, more fully.

In a way that only a mother can, Mary, our heavenly Mother, is close by and available, waiting to assist and guide us on our earthly and spiritual journey to her Son, Jesus.

Jesus Christ came to us through Mary—we can
go to Jesus through Mary.

To Mary, Queen of the Apostles

Most holy Mary, Queen of the Apostles and our
    model of prayer,
look with kindness upon the world, upon its
    people and leaders.
Help them, O Mary, to grow in their love of
    God and neighbor.
Queen of Peace, inspire all people to be truly
    grateful for the blessings of peace that they
    enjoy.
May they always live in harmony with one
    another.
We ask you to intercede for the many people
    who suffer from war, violence, injustice,
    oppression, and from social and economic
    hardship.
Chosen by God as a highly favored daughter
    "full of grace," you brought forth the Savior.
Open the hearts of all the peoples of the world
    to the dignity and vocation of every human
    person created and redeemed by God.

Mother of the Church, I entrust to you today
all the bishops, priests, men and women
religious.
Intercede for us and obtain an increase of
vocations to the priesthood and religious life.
Mother of Sorrows, at the foot of the cross you
never lost hope in God's power to save.
Be close to all who suffer: those with family
problems, the refugees, the poor, and the
unemployed.
Bring comfort to the sick and dying. May they
receive compassion from others and put all
their trust in God.
We turn to you, Mother, as our refuge and hope
on this our earthly pilgrimage.
You are the Queen of hope, and we entrust
ourselves to you this day.
As you once prayed for the promised gift of the
Holy Spirit in the midst of the apostles,
pray now for us, that through the power of the
same Spirit, we may truly be witnesses to
Christ, your Son. To him be glory forever.
Amen.

Saint John Paul II

To Mary Immaculate
for the Spread of the Gospel

O Mary Immaculate, you who gave birth to the
Word made flesh,

be present among us: assist, inspire, and comfort
the ministers of the word.

O Mary Immaculate, you who are the Queen of
the Apostles,

intervene with your protection that the light of
the Gospel may reach all peoples.

O Mary Immaculate, Mother of Jesus Way,
Truth, and Life,

intercede for us so that heaven may be filled

with those who sing the hymn of glory to the
most Holy Trinity. Amen.

Blessed James Alberione

Novena in Honor of Our Lady
of the Miraculous Medal

Immaculate Virgin Mary, conceived without sin,
you are the Mother of Jesus and my Mother. Through
the Miraculous Medal, you have encouraged us to
have great confidence in your intercession, and so I

now come to you in total trust to present to you my petition [*mention your request*]. Obtain for me also the grace of a holy life, that I may always give glory to God. Amen.

O Mary, conceived without sin, pray for us who have recourse to you [*say three times*].

Act of Consecration to Our Lady of the Miraculous Medal

O Virgin Mother of God, Mary Immaculate, I dedicate and consecrate myself to you under the title of Our Lady of the Miraculous Medal. May this medal be for me a sure sign of your affection and a constant reminder of my obligations toward you. Ever while wearing this medal, may I be blessed by your loving protection and preserved in the grace of your Son. O most powerful Virgin, Mother of our Savior, keep me close to you every moment of my life. Obtain for me, your child, the grace of a happy death, so that, together with you, I may enjoy the happiness of heaven forever. Amen.

O Mary, conceived without sin, pray for us who have recourse to you [*say three times*].

Novena in Honor of Our Lady of Fatima

Most holy Virgin, you appeared at Fatima to reveal to the three shepherd children the treasures of graces hidden in the recitation of the Rosary. Inspire my heart with a sincere love for this devotion, so that by meditating on the mysteries of our redemption that are recalled in it, I may gather their fruits and obtain the conversion of sinners and the special request I now make in this novena [*mention your request*], for the greater glory of God, for your honor, and for the good of all people. Amen.

Our Father, Hail Mary, Glory to the Father.

Our Lady of the Rosary of Fatima, pray for us.

Heart of Mary, be my salvation.

Thirty Days' Prayer to the Blessed Virgin Mary

Ever glorious and blessed Mary, Queen of Virgins and Mother of Mercy, you are the hope and comfort of those who suffer in body, mind, or spirit. Take pity on me, I implore you, because of the sword of sorrow that pierced your motherly heart as

your only Son, Jesus Christ, suffered disgrace and death on the cross. Take pity because of his most tender and pure love for you, grieving in your sorrows. From the cross he gave you to the care and protection of his beloved disciple, Saint John. I ask you, Mother, to have that same compassion on my anxieties and fears. Assist and comfort me in my time of illness and distress.

You are the Mother of Mercy, the gentle consoler and refuge of those impoverished, depressed, and troubled. Therefore, look upon me with pity and hear my prayer; I am surrounded by temptations and oppressed with anguish of spirit. Where can I find a more secure shelter, O Mother of my Lord and Savior Jesus Christ, than within the arms of your maternal protection? Listen, I beg you, with an ear of pity and compassion, to my humble and sincere request [*mention your petition*]. I ask it through the mercy of your Son, Jesus Christ, through that love and self-emptying with which he embraced our nature. In accord with the divine will you gave your consent, and after nine months you gave birth to Jesus that he might enter this world and bless it with his presence.

I ask your help through the anguish of mind that swept over your beloved Son, our dear Savior, on Mount Olivet. There he called upon his eternal

Father to remove the bitter chalice of his future passion. I ask your help through the threefold petition of our Savior's prayer in the garden, after which, amid sorrow and tears, you accompanied him to the place of his suffering and death.

I ask your help through the lashes and wounds to his flesh from the cords and whips with which he was bound and scourged when stripped of his seamless garment—for which the executioners cast lots. I ask it through the taunts and ridicule by which he was insulted. I ask it through the false accusations and unjust sentence by which he was condemned to death, and which he bore with the utmost patience. I ask it through his bitter tears and bloody sweat, his silence and resignation, his sadness and grief of heart. I ask it through the blood that flowed from his sacred head when struck with the scepter of a reed and pierced with a crown of thorns. I ask it through the excruciating pain he suffered when his hands and feet were fastened with large nails to the tree of the cross.

I ask your help through Jesus' intense thirst and bitter mixture of vinegar and gall. I ask it through his abandonment on the cross, when he exclaimed: "My God! My God! Why have you forsaken me?" I ask it through his mercy extended to the repentant

thief. I ask it through the giving over of his spirit into the hands of his eternal Father before he died, saying, "All is consummated." I ask it through the blood and water that spilled from his side when pierced with a lance, and from which grace and mercy flowed to us. I ask it through his blameless life and bitter passion. I ask it through his cruel death on the cross, at which nature itself rebelled through darkness and earthquake. I ask it through his descent among the dead, where he comforted the saints of the Old Law with his presence.

I ask your help through your Son's glorious victory when he suffered death, was buried, and rose again on the third day. I ask it through the joy his appearances for forty days after gave you, his blessed Mother, his Apostles, and his other disciples. I ask it through his miraculous ascension into heaven. I ask it through the grace the Holy Spirit poured out in the form of flaming tongues into the hearts of the disciples. I ask it through the grace by which the Apostles were inspired with zeal for the conversion of the world and went forth to preach the Gospel. I ask it through the awe-inspiring appearance of your Son on the last day, when he will come to judge the living and the dead. I ask it through the care and concern Jesus bore you in this life, and the indescribable joy you felt when you were taken up into heaven, where you are forever immersed in the contemplation of his divine perfections. O glorious and ever Blessed Virgin, console my heart by obtaining for me [*mention your request*].

I am convinced that my divine Savior honors you as his beloved Mother and will refuse you nothing—because you ask nothing contrary to God's will—so let me promptly experience the value of your powerful intercession and your maternal affection. May his heart, so loving toward his sons and daughters, mercifully grant my requests and fulfill the desires of all who love and revere him.

O most Blessed Virgin, I ask your intercession for my petition, and all else I need. I ask you also to obtain for me a lively faith, firm hope, ardent charity, true contrition of heart, the desire and strength to avoid sin, love of God and my neighbor, patience in the face of suffering, and even death for love of your Son, our Savior, Jesus Christ.

Obtain for me, as well, O holy Mother of God, victory over selfishness, perseverance in good works, realization of good resolutions, and holiness of life. During my last moments here on earth, grant me

wholehearted and sincere repentance. May my sorrow be accompanied by a lively presence of mind that will enable me to worthily receive the last sacraments of the Church and die in your friendship and favor. Lastly, I beseech you to obtain life everlasting for my parents, brothers and sisters, relatives, friends, and loved ones—both living and deceased. Amen.

Novena in Honor of the Immaculate Conception

Holy Mary, Immaculate Mother of God, before all the saints in heaven and with your devotees here on earth, I give my heart to you, weak and troubled as it may be. I beseech you to receive this offering of respect, love, and confidence as I come to you, my refuge in time of need. I ask you to intercede on my behalf with your Son, Jesus.

Present my petition to God and obtain for me [*mention your request*]. Protect me, O holy and Immaculate Mother of God, watch over me and guide me, now and forever. Amen.

Pray three Hail Marys, one Glory to the Father.

O Mary, conceived without sin, pray for us
    who have recourse to you.

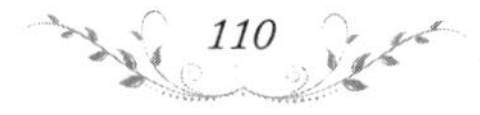

Novena in Honor of Our Lady of Perpetual Help

Behold, O Mother of Perpetual Help, I, a poor sinner, entrust myself to your never failing help.

O Mother of Mercy, you are the refuge and the hope of sinners. Be now my refuge and my hope. Assist me for the love of your Son, Jesus Christ, and intercede for me to obtain pardon for my sins, the strength to overcome temptations, and the grace to lead a holy life. God has blessed me with this confidence in you, to call upon you in every need, O Mother of Perpetual Help. Present my petition to Jesus [*mention your request*] and intercede for me now and always, that I may be received into the kingdom of heaven to be united with him forever. Amen.

Our Father, Hail Mary, Glory to the Father.

To the Immaculate Heart of Mary

O Mother of Jesus, and my Mother, let me dwell with you, cling to you, and love you with ever-increasing love.

I promise the honor, love, and trust of a child. Grant me a mother's protection, for I need your watchful care. You know better than any other the

thoughts and desires of the Sacred Heart. Keep constantly before my mind the same thoughts and the same desires, that my heart may be filled with dedication to the interests of the Sacred Heart of your divine Son. Fill me with a love of all that is noble, that I may not be easily turned to selfishness. Help me, dearest Mother, to acquire the virtues that God wants of me: to be self-forgetting, to work for him alone, without fear of sacrifice. I shall always rely on your help to be all that Jesus wants me to be. I am his; I am yours, my good Mother!

Give me each day your holy and maternal blessing until my last moment on earth, when your immaculate heart will present me to the heart of Jesus in heaven, there to love and praise you and your divine Son for all eternity. Amen.

Blessed John Henry Newman

To Our Lady of Sorrows

O Mother of Sorrows, Queen of Martyrs, you stood by the cross of your divine Son and endured with him the sorrows of his passion. Look with tenderness and pity on all mothers who suffer when their children undergo physical or emotional pain. Through the merits of your Son's sacred passion and death, together with your own sufferings, grant them your comfort and love.

Dearest Mother, intercede for me in my time of suffering [*mention your request*], that I may not lose heart but may remain steadfast in my devotion to your Son, Jesus. Grant that all I say and do may serve to praise and glorify God until the day I rejoice with you and all the saints and angels in heaven. Amen.

To Our Lady of Lourdes

O Immaculate Virgin, Mother of Mercy, Health of the Sick, Refuge of Sinners, Comforter of the Afflicted, no one who ever sought your help was left unaided.

You appeared in the Grotto of Lourdes and made it a sanctuary where you continue to dispense your favors to those who suffer from spiritual and corporal infirmities.

I come before you fully confident in your maternal intercession and ask that you hear my prayer and intercede for me [*mention your request*].

Grant me also the grace to imitate your virtues and persevere in leading a life of integrity and holiness.

Our Lady of Lourdes, pray for me and for all my loved ones. Amen.

To Our Lady of Guadalupe

Our Lady of Guadalupe, Mystical Rose, intercede for the holy Church, protect our Holy Father the Pope, and help all those who invoke you in time of need.

You are the ever Virgin Mary and Mother of God; therefore, obtain for us from your most holy Son the grace of keeping our faith. Give us burning charity, hope in the midst of the bitterness of life, and the precious gift of final perseverance. Amen.

To Our Lady of Mount Carmel

O most beautiful flower of Mount Carmel, fruitful vine, splendor of heaven, Blessed Mother of the Son of God, Immaculate Virgin, grant me your help in my necessity. O Star of the Sea, show me that you are my Mother. Holy Mary, Mother of God, Queen of heaven and earth, with confidence and love I place my petition in your hands and seek your intercession in my time of need [*mention your request*]. Amen.

O Mary, Our Lady of Mount Carmel, conceived without sin, pray for us who have recourse to you [*say three times*].

Sweet Mother, I place this cause in your hands [*say three times*].

Consecration to Our Lady

Hail Mary, Mother, Teacher, and Queen of angels and patriarchs, of apostles and martyrs, of confessors and virgins. From your throne in heaven you look down upon the earth, upon the just and the erring alike, ever concerned for the eternal salvation of all. You remember that Jesus, when dying on the cross, gave you to us as our Mother and poured into your heart a universal love and concern for all humanity. Therefore, continue to inspire, comfort, and form holy disciples who are self-giving followers of your divine Son.

And we, called to the Christian vocation and holiness of life, today consecrate to you all our undertakings and the fatigue of daily work. Above all, we consecrate to you ourselves: our strength, our intelligence, our will, our heart. We are all yours, and all that we are we offer to Jesus through you, dear Mother. Obtain for us an abundant outpouring of the Holy Spirit, as you did for the first apostles. Enlighten our minds to understand our vocation in life; fortify our wills; inflame our hearts; sanctify all that we do.

Grant that we may listen to, follow, and love Jesus Christ the Divine Master. May sin never stain our

souls consecrated to you, O Immaculate Virgin. Live in our midst, O Mary.

Speak to our hearts, O Jesus. Say your words of eternal life. Send forth your Spirit over the world so that there may be one teaching, one truth, one Master, one Faith, and one Church.

Come, Jesus, live in us and reign, through Mary and with Mary, over the world. Through you, Jesus; through you, Mary; glory to God throughout the ages, and on earth peace to all. Amen.

Blessed James Alberione

To Mary, Mother of Mercy

Virgin full of goodness, Mother of mercy,
> I entrust to you my body and my soul, my thoughts and my actions, my life and my death.

O my Queen, come to my aid and deliver me
> from the snares of evil.

Obtain for me the grace to love my Lord Jesus
> Christ, your Son, with a true and perfect love, and after him, O Mary, to love you with all my heart and above all things.

Amen.

Saint Thomas Aquinas

Ancient Prayer to the Virgin Mary

We fly to your protection,
O holy Mother of God.
Hear our petitions in our necessities,
and deliver us from all dangers,
O glorious and blessed Virgin.

Oldest known prayer to the Virgin,
found in a Greek papyrus, c. 300

Canticle of Mary

My soul gives praise to the Lord,
    and my spirit rejoices in God my Savior;
Because he had regard for the lowliness of his
        handmaid,
    behold, henceforth all generations shall call
        me blessed,
For the Mighty One has done great things for
    me,
    and holy is his name,
And his mercy is from generation to generation
    toward those who fear him.
He has shown might with his arm,
    scattered the arrogant in the conceit of their
        heart,

He has pulled down the mighty from their
    thrones,
    and exalted the lowly,
The hungry he has filled with good things,
    and the rich he has sent away empty.
He has come to the aid of his servant, Israel,
    mindful of his mercy,
Just as he promised our fathers,
    Abraham and his descendants forever.

Luke 1:46–55

To Mary of the Annunciation

May all generations proclaim you blessed, O
Mary.

You believed the words the Archangel Gabriel
spoke to you, and in you were fulfilled all the great
things he had announced.

My soul and my entire being praise you, O Mary.

You had faith in the incarnation of God's Son in
your virginal womb, and you became the Mother of
God.

Then the happiest day in human history dawned.
The world was given Jesus, the Son of God, the
Divine Teacher and King of the Universe.

Faith is a gift of God and the source of everything that is good. O Mary, obtain for us a lively, firm, and active faith—a faith that leads to holiness in this life and the assurance of eternal life in heaven.

May we ponder the words of your beloved Son and hold them in our hearts, just as you contemplated and preserved them in your heart.

May the Gospel be preached to the ends of the earth. May everyone believe the truth of its message so that all people will become, in Jesus Christ, children of God. Amen.

Blessed James Alberione

To Our Lady of the Assumption

O Immaculate Virgin, you are Mother of God and Mother of all people.

We believe with firm faith that you were assumed, body and soul, into heaven, where you reign as Queen of all the angels and saints. United with them, we praise and bless the Lord who has favored you above all creatures, as we offer you the tribute of our devotion and love.

We trust that in your goodness and mercy you are ever ready to assist us in time of weakness, sorrow,

and sadness. Strengthen us in time of temptation, and rejoice with us in our joys and our victories. Be our guide, strength, and consolation throughout this life's journey.

Grant your heavenly assistance and tender mercy to your suffering children throughout the world. Deliver them from the perils of war, persecution, hunger, and displacement. Comfort their aching hearts and weary bodies, and bring them to a place of safety and peace.

Comforted by our faith in God's promise of our future resurrection, we look to you, our life, our sweetness, and our hope. Draw us onward to that day, and after our exile here on earth, show us Jesus, the blessed fruit of your womb.

O clement, O loving, O sweet Virgin Mary. Amen.

Pope Pius XII

To Mary, Untier of Knots

Holy Mary, full of God's presence during the
    days of your life,
you accepted with full humility the Father's will,
and the devil was never able to tie you around
    with his confusion.

Once with your Son you interceded for our
     difficulties,
and, full of kindness and patience, you gave us
     an example of how to untie the knots of our
     life.
By remaining forever our Mother,
you put in order and make more clear the ties
     that link us to the Lord.
Holy Mother, Mother of God and our Mother,
who untie with a motherly heart the knots of
     our life, we pray to you to receive in your
     hands [*the person's name*],
and to free him/her of the knots and confusion
     with which our enemy attacks.
Through your grace, your intercession, and your
     example,
deliver us from all evil, our Lady, and untie the
     knots that prevent us from being united with
     God,
so that we, free from sin and error, may find him
     in all things,
may have our hearts placed in him,
and may serve him always in our brothers
     and sisters. Amen.

Pope Francis

PRAYERS TO
THE ANGELS

"I am going to send an angel in front of you, to guard you on the way and to bring you to the place that I have prepared" (Ex 23:20).

Many passages in Scripture refer to angels—beginning with the book of Genesis and through the Old and New Testaments. Sacred Scripture depicts the angels as helpers, protectors, and guides. They are ministers or messengers of God, whom God assigns to us as guardians and friends.

Angels are created spirits, neither male nor female, but real beings who possess a vast intellectual capacity and extraordinary strength of will. They are invisible, immortal, individual spirits who never age, whose strength never fails, and whose beauty never diminishes.

Artists depict angels with bodies to make them and their qualities of beauty and strength visible to us. Often angels are represented with wings to indicate their swiftness and eagerness to fulfill the will of God and also to symbolize their readiness to take our prayers and present them before the throne of the Most High.

We can invoke the help of the angels in all our spiritual and material needs. We can ask our guardian angel to intercede for us, to watch over us when we travel, to support us during difficult times, and to strengthen us in time of temptation. Since the Lord has so generously entrusted us to the care of the angels, we can respond in gratitude and be angels of consolation, joy, and goodness both to those around us and to those whom we meet.

TO SAINT GABRIEL THE ARCHANGEL

For a Special Intention

Blessed Saint Gabriel, Archangel, I beseech you to intercede for me at the throne of divine mercy in my present need. You are the angel of the Incarnation who was appointed by God to announce this wondrous mystery to Mary. Through your prayers may I receive a deepening of faith and a strengthening of spirit to strive wholeheartedly for holiness of life. Steady my resolutions and renew my courage. Console me in times of suffering and protect me in times of temptation, until the day I enjoy the fruits of redemption through Christ our Lord, and sing the praise of God forever in heaven. Amen.

For the Messengers of the Gospel

Saint Gabriel, you brought the good news of salvation to Mary; assist, inspire, and comfort the ministers of the word.

Saint Gabriel, you acted as the messenger of God; intervene with your protection, that the light of the Gospel may reach all peoples.

Saint Gabriel, you were the herald of Jesus, the Way, the Truth, and the Life; intercede for us, so that heaven may be filled with those who sing the hymn of glory to the Most Holy Trinity. Amen.

Blessed James Alberione

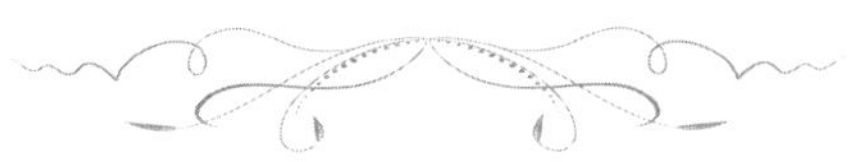

TO SAINT MICHAEL
THE ARCHANGEL

Protector of God's People

Saint Michael the Archangel, defend us in the battle. Be our defense against the wickedness and deceit of the devil. May God rebuke him, we humbly pray. And you, O prince of the heavenly host, by the power of God banish into hell Satan and the other evil spirits who roam through the world seeking the ruin of souls. Amen.

Pope Leo XIII

In Time of Difficulty

Glorious Saint Michael, prince of the heavenly host, valiant defender of the Church, you are always ready to assist the People of God in time of adversity. Be with me now in my hour of difficulty that I may walk steadfastly along the way of discipleship. I have confidence that through your intercession the Lord will grant me all the spiritual grace and strength that I need to follow Jesus more closely, and that one day I may rejoice forever with you in heaven. Amen.

For Police Officers

Saint Michael, defender against the forces of evil, protect our police officers and sustain them in their never-ending struggle to defeat criminal forces in our society. Ask the Lord to keep them safe and give them courage in the face of danger, right judgment in the face of confusion, and clarity in the face of ambiguity. Inspire them to safeguard human dignity, and keep their hearts free from anger and bitterness when confronted with so much wrongdoing.

Encourage them to be compassionate with those who are hurting, and give them self-control when confronting perpetrators. Be their constant companion and keep them safe from temptation and harm. Teach them how to live by faith in Jesus' promise that he is with us always. Teach them how to live in hope, relying on the Lord's saving power to bring them through hard times. Teach them how to live in Jesus' love, that they may be light in the darkness for others.

Trusting in your powerful intercession before the throne of God, I ask that you guide all law enforcement officers along life's journey, until the day they join you and all the angels in heaven to praise God for all eternity. Amen.

A Police Officer's Prayer

Saint Michael, defender against the forces of evil, protect all police officers and sustain us in our never-ending struggle to defeat criminal forces in our society. Ask the Lord to keep us safe and give us courage in the face of danger, right judgment in the face of confusion, and clarity in the face of ambiguity. Inspire us to safeguard human dignity, and keep our hearts free from anger and bitterness when confronted with so much wrongdoing.

Encourage us to be compassionate with those who are hurting, and give us self-control when confronting perpetrators. Be our constant companion and keep us safe from temptation and harm. Teach us how to live by faith in Jesus' promise that he is with us always. Teach us how to live in hope, relying on the Lord's saving power to bring us through hard times. Teach us how to live in Jesus' love, that we may be light in the darkness for others.

Trusting in your powerful intercession before the throne of God, I take you as my protector and guide along life's journey, relying on the Lord's loving care, that I may know his power working in my life until the day I join you and all the angels in heaven to praise God for all eternity. Amen.

To Saint Raphael
the Archangel

A Driver's Prayer

Heavenly Father, grant me a steady hand and a watchful eye, that I may safely reach my destination. Grant me self-control and freedom from aggressive behavior. Protect those who travel with me today. For those whom I drive or meet, let me be thoughtful and courteous so that I can, in some small way, mirror the love Jesus has for each of us. Open the eyes of my heart that I may see beyond the road and sky-scrapers to recognize the beauty that reflects the wonders of your creation.

Saint Raphael, Archangel, be my guide and protector today. Kindly precede me and guard me. Amen.

Blessed James Alberione

A Commuter's Prayer

Saint Raphael, Archangel, you brought healing, joy, and harmony to all those you met while you journeyed with young Tobiah. I, too, place myself under your protection as I commute today. Teach me how to be a bearer of God's healing peace as you were; let my words and actions reflect the kindness and compassion of Jesus. Be with me today and every day as I travel along the road of life. Amen.

For Travelers

Saint Raphael, Archangel, as you protected young Tobiah on his journey to a distant land, protect all those who travel today, especially [*name*]. Safeguard all fathers and mothers whose work requires them to travel; protect all children who travel to and from school or to be with a parent or visit a relative. Watch over those who journey to preach the Gospel. Guide those responsible for operating transport vehicles and inspire the owners of transportation systems to provide dependable and affordable means. Encourage those who maintain these systems to be trustworthy in providing safe and reliable means, so that all who travel will reach their destinations in comfort and safety. Amen.

For the Choice of a Spouse

Saint Raphael the Archangel, sent by God to counsel young Tobiah in the choice of a good and virtuous spouse, guide me too in this major life-choice. With your help I hope to meet the one who is "right for me," as a husband/wife. Through your inspiration I ask that my heart's choice might be the spouse the Lord would also choose for me, so that our life together will be one of mutual happiness and love. Amen.

TO THE GUARDIAN ANGELS

Daily Prayer

Angel of God, my guardian dear, to whom God's love entrusts me here; ever this day be at my side, to light and guard, to rule and guide. Amen.

For Protection

Father in heaven, I thank you for having entrusted me to an angel who will "light and guard, rule and guide" me always. I also thank you, my guardian angel, for accompanying me daily on my life's journey back to my heavenly Father. Your holy inspirations, your continual protection against both spiritual and bodily dangers, and your powerful prayers to God give me great comfort and sure hope. Amen.

Blessed James Alberione

PRAYERS TO THE SAINTS

The Communion of Saints—all the faithful of Christ—includes those still living on earth; those who have gone ahead in death, awaiting the moment they will enter into the happiness of heaven; and those in heaven enjoying the full presence of God. The Communion of Saints is like an extended family where the members help one another. We on earth assist the souls of the dead through our prayers and sacrifices, and the saints in heaven help us to be authentic followers of Jesus Christ and intercede for us in our times of need.

All the faithful in heaven are saints, but among them are those men and women the Church has publicly recognized for the practice of Christian virtue that is considered heroic. This heroic virtue is most often seen and practiced in quieter ways, like struggling with human frailties and foibles, always faithful to the calling received and following Christ day by day in faith, hope, and love.

Here on earth, we honor or venerate these persons as examples of virtue that we can imitate, and we ask them to pray for us. From the earliest centuries, the Church has encouraged believers to turn to the saints in heaven and to seek their intercession.

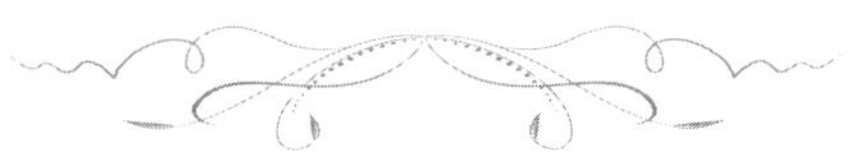

TO SAINT ANNE

For a Special Intention

Good Saint Anne, you were favored by God to be the mother of Mary, most holy, Mother of our Savior, Jesus Christ. Intercede now with your beloved daughter and with her divine Son, and obtain for me the grace I now seek [*mention your request*]. I ask forgiveness for all of my past sins, the strength to faithfully carry out my daily responsibilities, and the help I need to persevere in the love of Jesus and Mary. Amen.

In Time of Need

Glorious Saint Anne, filled with compassion for those who invoke you and with love for those who suffer, I kneel before you burdened by the weight of my troubles. I trustingly implore you to intercede for me and to take my present need under your protection [*state your request*].

Recommend my petition to your daughter, the Blessed Virgin Mary, and lay it before the throne of Jesus. Above all else, obtain for me the grace to one day meet God face to face, so that with you and Mary and all the angels and saints I may praise him through all eternity. Amen.

TO SAINT ANTHONY

For a Special Intention

Saint Anthony, most gentle and kind saint of great virtue and charity toward all God's creatures, during your life on earth you were blessed with extraordinary gifts. Through your hands our compassionate Lord granted health to the sick; through your efforts he restored what was lost to those who were searching; through your words he granted solace to anguished hearts.

Encouraged by the power of your intercession, I come to you with complete confidence and implore you to obtain from the Lord what I now ask [*mention your request*].

The answer to my prayer may require a miracle; yet, are you not the saint of miracles? O gentle and loving Saint Anthony, whose heart is ever full of human sympathy, take my prayer to the infant Jesus

for whom you have such great love. Speak to him for me, and the gratitude of my heart will ever be yours. Amen.

Our Father, Hail Mary, Glory to the Father.

To Recover Something Lost

Loving God, your have given us Saint Anthony as an intercessor for those who have lost material objects and things of spiritual value. With confidence in his prayers before your throne, I recommend to his intercession what I have lost [*mention what has been lost*]. If it be according to your will and for my greater spiritual well-being, I ask that it be restored to me. I ask this and all things through your Son, Jesus Christ. Amen.

For Every Need

Heavenly Father, you are ever praised and glorified in your servant Saint Anthony, whose intercessory power even today is a sign of your divine grace always at work in the world.

During his life on earth you gifted your servant Anthony with special favors and granted that even

from heaven he should continue to intercede for those who seek his help.

With confidence in your compassionate love, O Lord, I offer this prayer through the intercession of Saint Anthony and ask that you grant my request [*specify a special intention*].

Saint Anthony, pray for me and all my loved ones, that we may obtain the graces we need to be faithful followers of Jesus: to love God above all things, to love our neighbor as ourselves, to share with the poor unselfishly. Teach me, holy Saint Anthony, to walk the path of faith and to proclaim that faith in word and action, until the day I can join with you and all the saints to praise God forever in heaven.

I ask these and all spiritual blessings ✠ in the name of the Father, and of the Son, and of the Holy Spirit. Amen.

To Saint Blaise

For Illnesses of the Throat

O holy bishop and martyr Blaise, by your dedication to the spiritual needs of your people, and through your martyrdom, you have given the Church a valuable witness of courageous love and heroic faith. Obtain for me the grace to preserve the gift of faith I received at Baptism—that I may defend and uphold it in word and deed. Awaken within me the desire to reach out to those around me and to assist them in whatever way possible to me.

Saint Blaise, intercede for me to our Father in heaven to preserve me in soul and body, and deliver me especially from all illnesses of the throat. All these graces I ask through Jesus Christ, my Lord and Savior. Amen.

To Saint Brendan

For Navigators

Saint Brendan, holy navigator rightly called "God's Voyager," you courageously proclaimed the Gospel by means of long and exhausting sea journeys. Obtain for us the grace to welcome and treasure the message of salvation in Jesus Christ. Through your intercession may we be led safely through all the dangers of the sea until that day when we arrive at our final destination of heaven, where we will glorify God with you and all the saints. Amen.

TO SAINT CAMILLUS DE LELLIS

For Health Care Workers

Saint Camillus, special patron of the sick and their caregivers, intercede for all those who suffer and those who care for them. Grant to the sick faith-filled patience and enduring trust in the goodness and power of God. Grant to those who take care of them generosity of spirit and loving dedication. Lead me to better understand the mystery of suffering and to recognize it as a means to participate in the saving work of Jesus. Bestow your protection and comfort upon the sick and their families, and encourage them to live together in love. Bless all those who dedicate themselves to the care of the sick and suffering, and may God grant peace and hope to all. Amen.

To Saint Dymphna

For Someone Suffering from Depression

Almighty and eternal God, healer of those who trust in you, through the intercession of Saint Dymphna hear my prayer for [*name*]. In your tender mercy, lift the burden of depression from her/him and restore her/him to full emotional health, that she/he may give you thanks, praise your name, and proclaim your wondrous love to all. I ask this through Christ your Son, our Lord. Amen.

Our Father, Hail Mary, Glory to the Father.

For Health of Mind and Body

Compassionate Saint Dymphna, through the power of your heavenly Spouse, Jesus Christ, you granted health of mind and body to all who called upon you in their need. With a humble, trustful heart, and with faith in the Lord's healing power, I ask through your intercession to be restored to mental health and/or emotional well-being. Confident in the Lord's promise that whatever is asked in Jesus' name will be granted, I praise God for the many blessings I have already received from his generous love, and I look to the day when I can glorify him with you and all the saints in heaven. Amen.

Our Father, Hail Mary, Glory to the Father.
Saint Dymphna, pray for me.

For Those Suffering from Mental or Emotional Illness

Lord Jesus Christ, you have willed that Saint Dymphna should be invoked by her devotees as patroness of those who suffer from mental or emotional illness. You have also willed that her protective interest in these persons should be an inspiration to all believers and an ideal of charity for caregivers. Grant that, through the prayers of this youthful martyr, all those who suffer from mental and/or psychological illnesses may be helped and consoled. In particular I recommend to you [*mention those you wish to pray for*].

Divine Healer, be pleased to hear the prayers of Saint Dymphna and of your Blessed Mother, health of the sick and comforter of the afflicted, on behalf of those whom I recommend to the love and compassion of your Sacred Heart. Give them the consolation they need and, if it be your will, the healing they so much desire. May we all serve your suffering members with selfless love until the day we are united forever in heaven with you, who live and reign with the Father in the unity of the Holy Spirit, forever and ever. Amen.

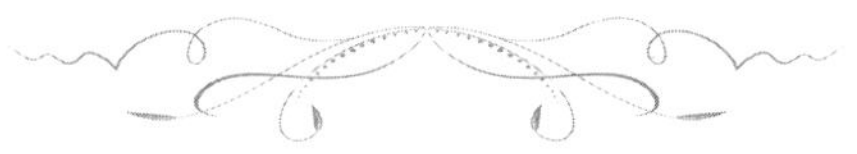

To Saint Florian

For Firefighters and First Responders

Father in heaven, through the intercession of Saint Florian, grant your mercy to all those who have lost their lives in the performance of their duty, and all those who have gone before us after years of faithful service. Give us the grace to live each day under your protection and guidance, ready and willing to do good to all people.

Merciful Lord, save us all from bodily harm, but, above all, help us to be loyal and true, respectful and honorable, virtuous and valiant. Fortified by your grace, we want to live in your love with the hope that one day we will be with you forever in heaven. Amen.

TO SAINT FRANCIS OF ASSISI

For a Special Intention

O beloved Saint Francis, in your youth you renounced the comfort and ease of your father's house and with a generous heart chose to follow Jesus more closely in his humility, poverty, and self-sacrifice. Obtain for me, I pray, the grace to pass through this life ever more convinced of the short-lived satisfaction gained from earthly possessions. Direct my thoughts and desires toward a deep love for Jesus crucified, that I may lead a life of goodness and service of others.

From your place among the saints in heaven, I ask that you intercede for me and present my special request to God [*mention your request*]. All glory and praise to God, the Father, the Son, and the Holy Spirit. Amen.

To Saint Francis Xavier

Novena of Grace

This novena usually begins on March 4 and closes on March 12, cele-brating the canonization of Saint Ignatius Loyola and Saint Francis Xavier. Or it may be prayed from November 25 to December 3, the feast of Saint Francis Xavier.

Most kind and loving Saint Francis Xavier, in union with you I humbly adore the most divine Majesty. With you I offer praise and thanksgiving to God for the gifts of grace he bestowed upon you during your life, and the gifts of glory after your death.

Through your powerful intercession I ask you to obtain for me the grace to live a holy life and to die a happy and peaceful death. Moreover, I ask you to obtain for me the favor I seek in this novena [*mention your request*].

But if what I ask is not for the greater glory of God and the greater good of my soul, obtain for me the graces that are most beneficial to both these ends. Amen.

Our Father, Hail Mary, Glory to the Father.

To Saint Genesius

Patron Saint of Actors and Entertainers

O holy Saint Genesius, martyr for Christ, by the grace of God you came to discover the truth of the Christian faith through your acting.

In your profession of that faith you were baptized through the shedding of your blood, offering your life for the praise and glory of our Lord Jesus Christ.

Pray for those who devote their lives to theater entertainment, film, and the performing arts. In their work may they find the presence of God and generously open their hearts to the teaching of Jesus Christ, and may they live it in the midst of the challenges and demands of their profession.

Intercede for actors and entertainers, especially [*mention the name*], so that the same grace you received may be given to those who as yet do not know Jesus Christ. May those who have heard and believe be renewed and strengthened in their faith. We ask this through Christ our Lord. Amen.

To Saint Gerard

For a Special Intention

Saint Gerard, you loved God and served him faithfully while on earth. Now from heaven teach me to have great confidence in the Lord and to recognize his faithful love in my life.

Trusting in your powerful intercession before the most Blessed Trinity, I ask you to obtain this favor [*mention your request*]. I believe there is no limit to what God can do, and I place my faith in his infinite wisdom and goodness, always at work even when I cannot see or understand it. I ask you to guide me along life's journey until the day I will join you and all the angels and saints in heaven to praise God for all eternity. Amen.

Our Father, Hail Mary, Glory to the Father.

For Motherhood

Saint Gerard, powerful intercessor before God, I come to ask your help. Beseech the Lord, the Giver of all life, to grant me the grace to conceive a child, if it be according to his plan. I hope to bear children who will be faith-filled disciples of Jesus, witnesses to his message of love, and heirs to the kingdom of heaven. Amen.

For an Expectant Mother

Almighty and loving God, through the power of the Holy Spirit you prepared the Virgin Mary to be the worthy bearer of your own Son, Jesus. Listen to my prayer through the intercession of Saint Gerard, your faithful servant, and protect [*name*] during her pregnancy and birthing.

Creator of Life, grant [*name*] the joy of anticipating new life within her womb, and in time of pain or distress allow her to experience your consoling presence. Grant her, Lord, the spiritual and emotional care she needs in order to bring her child into the world. Give [*name*] the wisdom to know how to safeguard her physical welfare, so that the child she carries within her may be healthy in mind and body. May all of her children bring her joy and reflect your love for her, until they may one day enjoy the eternal happiness of heaven. Amen.

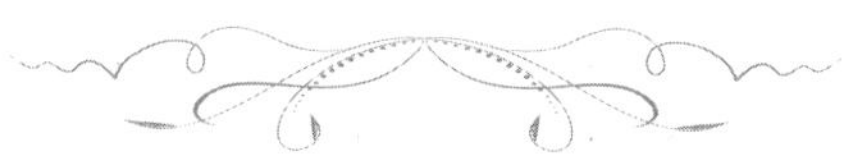

To Saint Joseph

To Obtain a Special Favor

O glorious Saint Joseph, steadfast follower of Jesus Christ, I am confident that your prayers for me will be graciously heard at the throne of God. To you I lift my heart and hands, asking your powerful intercession to obtain from the compassionate heart of Jesus all the graces necessary for my spiritual and temporal well-being, particularly the grace of a happy death, and the special grace for which I now pray [*mention your request*].

Saint Joseph, Guardian of the Word Incarnate, by the love you bear for Jesus Christ, and for the glory of his name, hear my prayer and obtain my petitions. Amen.

In Time of Need

Saint Joseph, patron of all who serve God in simplicity of heart and steadfast devotion, ask the Lord to fill my heart with the fire of his love. Awaken within me the virtues of integrity, simplicity, reverence, and gentleness, so that I may radiate God's love to those around me. Intercede for me in my time of particular need and obtain for me the favor I ask [*mention your request*]. Blessed Joseph, be my protector in life and my consoler at the moment of death. Amen.

For One's Family

Heavenly Father, I thank you for the gift of my family and for the many joys and blessings that have come to me through each of them. Help me to appreciate the uniqueness of each while celebrating the diversity of all. Through the intercession of Saint Joseph, foster father of your Son, I ask you to protect my family from the evils of this world. Grant all of us the power to forgive when we have been hurt, and the humility to ask for forgiveness when we have caused pain. Unite us in the love of your Son, Jesus, that we may be a sign of the unity you desire for all humankind.

Saint Joseph, intercede for us. Amen.

For Someone Seeking Employment

Saint Joseph, foster father of Jesus and spouse of the Virgin Mary, help me to find suitable work, with adequate pay and health benefits. You know the anxiety that I feel as I search for means to support myself and those who depend on me. I am confident that you understand my need to pay my just debts with dignity, and to help others who are also in need.

Holy Joseph, saint of divine Providence, teach me to trust in God as a loving Father, and intercede to God for me in all my needs. Amen.

A Worker's Prayer

Saint Joseph, example for all those who work to support themselves and their families, obtain for me the grace to labor with thankfulness and joy. Grant that I may consider my daily endeavors as opportunities to use and develop the gifts of nature and grace I have received from God. In the workplace may I mirror your virtues of integrity, moderation, patience, and inner peace, treating my co-workers with kindness and respect. May all I do and say lead others to the Lord and bring honor to God's name. Amen.

Memorare to Saint Joseph

Remember, O most chaste spouse of the Virgin Mary, that never has it been known that anyone who asked for your help or sought your intercession was left unaided. Inspired by this confidence, I commend myself to you and beg your protection. Despise not my petition, dear foster father of our Redeemer, but hear and answer my prayer. Amen.

Prayer for a Happy Death

Saint Joseph, protector of the dying, I ask you to intercede for all the dying and invoke your assistance in the hour of my own death. You merited a happy passing by a holy life, and in your last hours you had the great consolation of being assisted by Jesus and Mary. Deliver me from sudden death; obtain for me the grace to imitate you in life, to detach my heart from everything worldly, and daily to gather treasures for the moment of my death. Obtain for me the grace to receive the sacraments of the sick, and with Mary, fill my heart with sentiments of faith, hope, love, and sorrow for sins, so that I may breathe forth my soul in peace. Amen.

Blessed James Alberione

To Saint Jude

To Obtain a Special Favor

Glorious apostle Saint Jude Thaddeus, I praise the infinite mercy of God and thank him for the countless gifts he has bestowed on men and women throughout the ages. God has granted you the grace and privilege to give help in desperate cases, so I turn to you with a humble and trustful heart. Look upon me with compassion; come to my aid and intercede for me before our gracious God in this my time of need [*mention your request*]. I take you as my protector and guide along life's journey, relying on the Lord's loving care that I may know his power working in my life. Amen.

For Help in Time of Need

Saint Jude, faithful disciple and friend of Jesus, many have forgotten you because of the name of the man who betrayed his Master. But the Church honors you, most holy apostle, and invokes you as the universal patron of hopeless cases—of things despaired of. I ask you to intercede for me now in my time of need. Please bring help where help is almost despaired of, that I may receive consolation from the Lord in my suffering and assistance in my distress, particularly [*make your request*]. Trusting in the Lord's promise that whatever is asked in Jesus' name will be granted, I praise God for the many blessings I have already received from his generous love, and I look to the day when I can glorify him with all the saints in heaven. Amen.

In Time of Adversity

Saint Jude Thaddeus, glorious apostle and martyr, you are a faithful friend to all who rely on your intercession. Gracious patron and helper in time of adversity, I come to seek your help [*mention your request*]. The cross that I carry seems too heavy for me to bear; I feel anxious and discouraged in the face of this difficulty. Intercede for me, that I may once again know the power of the Lord's redeeming love and the shield of his comfort in my life. Teach me, gracious patron, how to live by faith in Jesus' promise that he is with me always. Teach me how to live in hope, relying on the Lord's saving power to bring me through this time of pain and suffering. Teach me how to live in love, that I may be a light in the darkness for others.

Glory to the Father.

For Someone Who Is Sick

Almighty and eternal God, healer of those who trust in you, through the intercession of Saint Jude hear my prayer for [*name*]. In your tender mercy restore her/him to bodily health, that she/he may give you thanks, praise your name, and proclaim your wondrous love to all. I ask this through Christ your Son, our Lord. Amen.

To Saint Lucy

To Obtain a Special Favor

Saint Lucy, virgin and martyr,
— intercede for us to God.

You were a faithful disciple of Jesus and a loving
servant of those in need,
— present my prayer of praise and supplication
to God.

God of goodness and mercy, I praise and thank
you for the many blessings I have received through
your generous love. As we honor your servant, Saint
Lucy, for the light of faith you granted her, I ask
that you increase and safeguard this same light
within me. Grant that I may spend my life doing
good and avoiding all that is not in accord with
your will for me.

Trusting in your goodness and with confidence in
your power to heal, I humbly ask, through the intercession of Saint Lucy, for this grace: [*mention your*

specific intention]. May all nations come to know the power of your love and the unfailing gift of your mercy, so that we may one day glorify you with all the saints in heaven. Amen.

Our Father, Hail Mary, Glory to the Father.

Saint Lucy, virgin and martyr, hear my prayers and answer my petition.

For Healing

Almighty and eternal God, healer of those who trust in you, through the intercession of Saint Lucy hear my prayer for [*name*]. In your tender mercy restore her/him to spiritual and/or bodily health, that she/he may give you thanks, praise your name, and proclaim your wondrous love to all. I ask this through Christ your Son, our Lord. Amen.

For Those Suffering From Eye Disease

Saint Lucy, whose name signifies light, to you I come full of confidence. I ask you to obtain for me a holy light that will prevent me from walking in the path of sin or from remaining surrounded by the darkness of error. I ask also, through your intercession, that God may heal the illness in my eyes, preserve the light of my eyes, and grant me an abundance of grace that I may use my sight according to the divine will. Grant, O Saint Lucy, that after venerating and thanking you for your powerful protection here on earth, I may finally share your joy in heaven in the eternal light of the Lamb of God, your beloved Bridegroom, our Lord Jesus Christ. Amen.

For Preservation of the Gift of Sight

O blessed and beloved Saint Lucy, I beseech you to ask the Lord Jesus to protect the light of my eyes, that I may make good use of them for the well-being of my soul. Obtain for me the grace that my mind may never be troubled nor my imagination filled with dangerous images. May all I look upon be holy and healthy food for my spirit, so that I may daily grow in love for my Creator and Redeemer, Jesus Christ. Through your intercession I hope to see and love him forever in heaven. Amen.

TO SAINT MARIA GORETTI

For the Virtue of Purity

We greet you, O beautiful and amiable saint: martyr on earth and saint in heaven. From your glory in heaven, look upon the people who love and venerate you.

As a martyr you bear on your forehead the radiant and victorious name of Jesus Christ. Your purity of heart allows us to see the strength of your love and the constancy of your fidelity to him.

O powerful intercessor with the Lamb of God, to you we entrust our sons and daughters, who, while they admire your heroism, are even more eager to imitate your strong faith and steadfast purity of conduct. Parents have recourse to you, asking you to help them in their task of educating their children.

In you may all young people find safe refuge, trusting that they will be protected from every toxic influence and be able to walk the highways of life with that serenity of spirit and deep joy that are the heritage of those who are pure of heart. Amen.

Pope Pius XII on the occasion of the canonization

To Saint Martha

For a Special Intention

O blessed Saint Martha, together with your sister, Mary, and your brother, Lazarus, you treasured the friendship of Jesus while he was on earth. Your deep faith let you see beyond his humanity, and you declared, "Lord, you are the Messiah, the Son of God." Your firm hope that God would give you whatever you asked of him prompted Jesus to call Lazarus back from the dead.

Teach me, Saint Martha, how to always hold God in my heart, to place my trust in him and speak of his goodness and mercy to others.

In your compassion continue to intercede for those who seek your help; with confidence in your prayers to God, I ask that you obtain for me all the graces necessary for my spiritual welfare and a particular favor at this time [*mention your special intention*].

Our Father, Hail Mary, Glory to the Father.

To Saint Martin de Porres

In Time of Need

Glorious Saint Martin de Porres, we thank and praise God for your inspiring example of charity. Your self-sacrificing love embraced sick, suffering, poor, and needy persons. Your concern for all God's creatures moved you to care for even the smallest and weakest animals of the field.

From your place in heaven among the saints, intercede to God for us who invoke you in our time of need [*mention your petition*]. By imitating your examples of charity, goodness, and patience, may we have the grace to accept the difficulties and sufferings of life, relying also on the help of Mary, our Blessed Mother. May we know and feel that Jesus is with us in our pain, bringing us healing and hope. May the trials we face not blind us to the many blessings we also receive from the hands of our heavenly Father as we look forward to the joys of heaven. Amen.

For Harmony Among Peoples

Saint Martin, your love for all of God's people gives us confidence to ask you to intercede for us, so that men and women of every ethnic group may value the gifts of culture and tradition that each possesses. May we act only and always with respect, kindness, and tolerance toward one another, doing our utmost to preserve the unity among peoples that the Spirit gives through the gift of peace and reconciliation. Amen.

Praise and Thanksgiving

Lord Jesus, I praise, glorify, and bless you for all the graces and privileges you have bestowed upon your servant and friend, Martin de Porres. By his merits grant me your grace, and through his intercession help me in all my needs. At the hour of my death be with me, until that time when I can join the saints in heaven to praise you forever and ever. Amen.

TO SAINT MONICA

For a Wayward Son or Daughter

Saint Monica, mother of Saint Augustine, you are a model of motherly love and tireless devotion. Who better than you can understand the anxieties and fears of a mother who worries over the spiritual well-being of her children? The conversion of your son was the fruit of your prayers and tears of suffering endured for his moral welfare.

Now, from heaven, intercede with our heavenly Father for [*mention the name*] and all sons and daughters who have wandered away from God. Pray for all those mothers worried about their children; strengthen and console them until the day they and their children enjoy the happiness of heaven with you and all the saints. Amen.

To Saint Paul

For Patience

Glorious Saint Paul, from a persecutor of Christianity you became an ardent apostle and evangelizer. Throughout your life you even suffered imprisonment, scourging, stoning, and shipwreck; you endured persecutions of every kind for the sake of the Gospel. Your sole desire was to make the Savior, Jesus Christ, known to the farthest bounds of the world, and to that end you shed your blood to the last drop.

Obtain for me the grace to accept the hardships of ill health and the daily struggles of this present life as opportunities to grow in love for Jesus Christ and share in his sufferings. May the unexpected difficulties that come my way help me to be a more patient, compassionate, and loving person who seeks to assist others in their needs. And, amid the pressures and

demands of everyday life, grant me enduring strength
to be a faithful and fervent follower of Jesus Christ.
Amen.

Blessed James Alberione

To Obtain a Special Favor

O holy Apostle, who preached the saving message of Christ and taught men and women how to
live in faith, hope, and love, intercede for us that we
may imitate your docility to God's will and corre-
spond to God's grace working in us.

Grant that we may ever better know you, love
you, and imitate you in your love for Jesus, our
Master, and in your dedication to proclaiming the
Gospel of salvation; that we may be living members
of the Church, the Mystical Body of Jesus Christ;
and that all people may know and glorify God.

Lord Jesus, in your mercy grant that, through the
powerful intercession of Saint Paul, we may obtain
the favor we ask at this time [*mention your petition*].
Amen.

Our Father, Hail Mary, Glory to the Father.
Saint Paul, the Apostle, pray for us.

Blessed James Alberione

For Our Nation

Saint Paul, preacher and apostle, watch over with love this nation and its people. Your heart opened out to welcome and enfold all peoples in the embrace of peace.

Now, from heaven, enlighten the people of this nation and its leaders with the light of the Gospel in order to establish the kingdom of love among those of every race, creed, and culture.

May this nation ever more find in Christ the Way and the Truth and the Life, and may it always seek the kingdom of God and his justice.

Holy Apostle, enlighten, comfort, and bless us all. Amen.

Blessed James Alberione

To Saint Peregrine

To Obtain a Special Favor

Good and gracious God, you gave Saint Peregrine an angel as his companion, the Mother of God as his teacher, and Jesus as his healer. Grant that I too may love and reverence my guardian angel; that I may love and venerate the Blessed Mother; and that I may ever seek to praise and worship Jesus, my Savior, until I am with them in heaven for all eternity.

Compassionate Lord, giver of all good things, through the intercession of Saint Peregrine grant me the graces that you know I need most at this time, and grant especially that [*mention your request*]. I ask this and all things through Christ, your Son. Amen.

For Someone with Cancer

Almighty and eternal God, healer of those who trust in you, through the intercession of Saint

Peregrine hear my prayer for [*name*]. In your tender mercy, restore her/him to bodily health, that she/he may give you thanks, praise your name, and proclaim your wondrous love to all. I ask this through Christ your Son, our Lord. Amen.

To Saint Pio of Pietrelcina

To Obtain a Special Favor

God of heaven and earth, in your infinite generosity you blessed your servant, Saint Pio of Pietrelcina, with the gifts of the Spirit. You marked his body with the five wounds of Christ Crucified as a witness to the saving power of your Son's passion and death.

You endowed him with the gift of discernment and the strength to spend endless hours in the confessional laboring continually for the salvation of souls.

Through reverence and intense devotion while celebrating Mass, he invited countless men and women to a greater union with Jesus Christ in the sacrament of the Holy Eucharist.

O Lord, through the intercession of Saint Pio of Pietrelcina, I confidently beseech you to grant me

the grace I ask for at this time [*mention your request*].
Amen.

Glory to the Father . . . (*three times*).

Prayer of Saint John Paul II

Saint Pio, teach us, we pray, humility of heart so that we may be counted among the little ones of the Gospel to whom the Father promised to reveal the mysteries of his kingdom.

Help us to pray without ceasing, certain that God knows what we need even before we ask him.

Obtain for us the eyes of faith that will help us recognize in the poor and suffering the very face of Jesus.

Sustain us in the hour of trouble and trial and, if we fall, let us experience the joy of the sacrament of forgiveness.

Grant us your tender devotion to Mary, Mother of Jesus and our Mother.

Accompany us on our earthly pilgrimage toward the blessed homeland where we too hope to arrive to contemplate forever the glory of the Father, the Son, and the Holy Spirit. Amen.

On the occasion of Saint Pio's canonization

To Saint Rita

In Time of Need

Weighed down with the burden of suffering, I turn to you, Saint Rita, "Saint of the Impossible," in the hope of receiving your immediate support. I ask you to free my heart from its many worries and give peace to my troubled spirit. Intercede to God for me as the advocate of the desperate; and if my sins are an obstacle to the realization of my petition, please obtain for me God's forgiveness.

Stem the flow of my tears and reward my steadfast hope, that I may give testimony to your compassion for all those who suffer distress and misfortune.

O loving companion of Christ Crucified, intercede for me now and forever. Amen.

For a Special Intention

Holy patroness of those in need, you suffered through a long illness and showed your love for Jesus Crucified through patient forbearance. Teach me how to pray so that I may join my sufferings with those of Jesus.

Filled with confidence in your intercession, I ask that you come to the aid and relief of [*name*] in their time of need. Trusting that all things are possible to God, I place my petition in your hands, that this healing may give glory to God and proclaim his love to the ends of the earth. Amen.

To Saint Sebastian

For Those in the Armed Forces

Holy Sebastian, soldier and martyr, strong in body and courageous in faith, protect all who serve in the Armed Forces. Defend them from all harm and keep them safe until the day they all return home to their families and loved ones. Like you, may they be temperate in all things, diligent in their duties, and patient in suffering. Be their guide along life's path, so that they may be prompt in doing good to all people, upright in all their dealings, and compassionate to everyone they meet.

Saint Sebastian, intercede for our men and women who serve in the Armed Forces. Amen.

To Saint Thérèse of Lisieux

For a Special Intention

Saint Thérèse, during your short life on earth you became a model of spiritual transparency, of love as strong as death, and of wholehearted abandonment to God. Now, from heaven, ask these same spiritual gifts for me and intercede for the special intention I place in your care [*mention your request*]. Present my petition to Mary, Queen of Heaven, for I trust that in her motherly affection she will bring my request to her Son, Jesus. I ask this and all spiritual blessings in the name of the Father, and of the Son, and of the Holy Spirit. Amen.

Our Father, Hail Mary, Glory to the Father.

For Help in Time of Need

Saint Thérèse, radiant flower that flourished in the garden of Carmel, I thank you for the love of God and concern for humankind that led you to

embrace a life of prayer and penance. How deep a debt of gratitude I owe you for the graces you have already obtained for me and for the world. I ask you now, once again, to intercede for me in my time of need, that the Lord may grant the grace I now ask [*mention your request*]. Watch over me, that I may grow in holiness; protect those whom I love and those for whom I pray. Trusting in Jesus' promise that whatever is asked in his name will be granted, I praise and thank God for his generous love, and I look to the day when I can glorify him with you and all the saints in heaven. Amen.

Our Father, Hail Mary, Glory to the Father.

For the Needs of the Church

Saint Thérèse, while on earth your desire was to live for Jesus alone, to undergo suffering for his sake, to make his Gospel message better known, and to make him loved by all. Now from heaven continue to send upon the world a shower of roses, spiritual favors that will inspire all persons to know that the passing things of this world cannot compare to the joys that await us in heaven.

For the Pope, ask the Lord to grant him the grace he needs to govern the Church with wisdom and

love. For the bishops, obtain for them the spiritual gifts necessary to be true shepherds of the flocks given to their care. For priests, ask God to give them the courage they need to meet the challenges of their vocation. For men and women religious, ask that they be granted enthusiasm for their calling and a loving reverence for all those whom they serve in their varied ministries. For the laity in the Church, ask for the gift of fidelity to Christ and to their call to discipleship. For those who have distanced themselves from the Church, inspire them to undertake the interior journey that will lead them back to the grace of the sacraments. For all Christians, ask for the gift of unity, and ask the Holy Spirit to inspire the hearts of all people to continue the saving work of Christ until the end of time, when we will all be united in heaven. Amen.

For Missionaries

Saint Thérèse of the Child Jesus, although you never left the seclusion of Carmel, you have been proclaimed the patroness of Catholic missions throughout the world. By the grace of the burning desire you had to preach the Gospel to the ends of the earth, I ask you to safeguard all missionaries. Ask the Lord to grant them courage and strength in the face of adversity, wisdom and zeal in proclaiming God's name among the nations, and fidelity and joy as his heralds of truth. Amen.

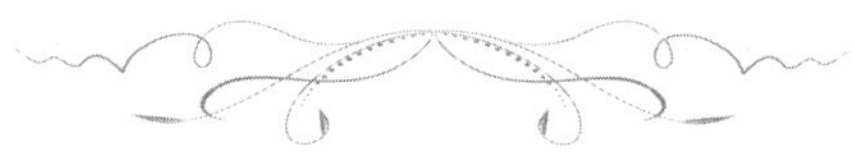

To Saint Thomas Aquinas

Novena Prayer

Saint Thomas Aquinas, patron of students and a model for teachers, I thank God for the gifts of enlightenment and knowledge he bestowed on you. I thank God also for the wealth and richness of your theological teaching and for the writings you left to enrich the Church's legacy of sacred literature. Not only were you a great teacher, you also lived a life of virtue and made holiness the desire of your heart. While I may not be able to imitate your brilliance in academic pursuits, I can follow your example of humility and charity.

Intercede for me, that I might grow in holiness of life and in charity, the greatest and lasting gift. Pray for all students, that in their pursuit of learning they may value moral standards in order to become leaven in society and promote respect for the dignity of human life at every stage. In particular, I ask your intercession for the special grace I seek at this time [*mention your request*]. Amen.

To My Patron Saint

For Protection

Heavenly Father, through the intercession of [*mention your patron saint*] I ask you to guard me against every danger of soul and body. Deliver me from every evil and direct me along the path of holiness, until the day I am united with you and all the saints in heaven. Amen.

Litany of the Saints

Lord, have mercy on us.

Christ, have mercy on us.

Lord, have mercy on us.

Christ, hear us.

Christ, graciously hear us.

God, the Father of heaven, *have mercy on us.*

God the Son, Redeemer of
    the world, *have mercy on us.*

God the Holy Spirit, *have mercy on us.*

Holy Trinity, one God, *have mercy on us.*

Holy Mary, *pray for us.*

Holy Mother of God, *pray for us.*

Holy Virgin of virgins, *pray for us.*

Saint Michael, *pray for us.*

Saint Gabriel, *pray for us.*

Saint Raphael, *pray for us.*

All you holy angels and archangels, *pray for us.*

All you holy orders of blessed spirits, *pray for us.*
Saint John the Baptist, *pray for us.*
Saint Joseph, *pray for us.*
All you holy patriarchs and prophets, *pray for us.*
Saint Peter, *pray for us.*
Saint Paul, *pray for us.*
Saint Andrew, *pray for us.*
Saint James the Greater, *pray for us.*
Saint John, *pray for us.*
Saint Thomas, *pray for us.*
Saint James the Lesser, *pray for us.*
Saint Philip, *pray for us.*
Saint Bartholomew, *pray for us.*
Saint Matthew, *pray for us.*
Saint Simon, *pray for us.*
Saint Thaddeus, *pray for us.*
Saint Matthias, *pray for us.*
Saint Barnabas, *pray for us.*
Saint Luke, *pray for us.*
Saint Mark, *pray for us.*
All you holy apostles and evangelists, *pray for us.*
All you holy disciples of the Lord, *pray for us.*
All you holy innocents, *pray for us.*
Saint Stephen, *pray for us.*

Saint Lawrence,   *pray for us.*
Saint Vincent,   *pray for us.*
Saints Fabian and Sebastian,   *pray for us.*
Saints John and Paul,   *pray for us.*
Saints Cosmos and Damian,   *pray for us.*
Saints Gervase and Protase,   *pray for us.*
All you holy martyrs,   *pray for us.*
Saint Sylvester,   *pray for us.*
Saint Gregory,   *pray for us.*
Saint Ambrose,   *pray for us.*
Saint Augustine,   *pray for us.*
Saint Jerome,   *pray for us.*
Saint Martin,   *pray for us.*
Saint Nicholas,   *pray for us.*
All you holy bishops and confessors,   *pray for us.*
All you holy doctors,   *pray for us.*
Saint Anthony,   *pray for us.*
Saint Benedict,   *pray for us.*
Saint Bernard,   *pray for us.*
Saint Dominic,   *pray for us.*
Saint Francis,   *pray for us.*
All you holy priests and friars,   *pray for us.*
All you holy monks and hermits,   *pray for us.*
Saint Mary Magdalene,   *pray for us.*

Saint Agatha,	*pray for us.*
Saint Lucy,	*pray for us.*
Saint Agnes,	*pray for us.*
Saint Cecilia,	*pray for us.*
Saint Catherine,	*pray for us.*
Saint Anastasia,	*pray for us.*
Saint Clare,	*pray for us.*
All you holy virgins and widows,	*pray for us.*
All you holy men and women, saints of God,	*intercede for us.*
Be merciful,	*spare us, O Lord.*
Be merciful,	*graciously hear us, O Lord.*
From all evil,	*Lord, deliver us.*
From all sin,	*Lord, deliver us.*
From sudden and violent death,	*Lord, deliver us.*
From the snares of the devil,	*Lord, deliver us.*
From hatred and hostility,	*Lord, deliver us.*
From natural disasters,	*Lord, deliver us.*
From earthquakes and hurricanes,	*Lord, deliver us.*
From sickness, famine, and war,	*Lord, deliver us.*
From everlasting death,	*Lord, deliver us.*
By the mystery of your Incarnation,	*Lord, deliver us.*
By your birth,	*Lord, deliver us.*
By your baptism and holy fasting,	*Lord, deliver us.*

By your cross and passion,   *Lord, deliver us.*
By your death and burial,   *Lord, deliver us.*
By your holy resurrection,   *Lord, deliver us.*
By your admirable ascension,   *Lord, deliver us.*
By the coming of the Holy Spirit,
    the Paraclete,   *Lord, deliver us.*
In the day of judgment,   *Lord, deliver us.*
Although we are sinners,   *we beseech you, hear us.*
That you pardon us,   *we beseech you, hear us.*
That you bring us to true
    repentance,   *we beseech you, hear us.*
That you govern and guard
    your holy Church,   *we beseech you, hear us.*
That you watch over the
    Pope and bishops,   *we beseech you, hear us.*
That you grant peace and true
    harmony among nations,   *we beseech you, hear us.*
That you deign to provide
    and preserve the fruits
    of the earth,   *we beseech you, hear us.*
That you grant peace and
    unity to all Christians,   *we beseech you, hear us.*
That you confirm and preserve
    us in your holy service,   *we beseech you, hear us.*

That you lift our minds and
hearts to heavenly desires,   *we beseech you, hear us.*
That you grant eternal blessings
to all our benefactors,   *we beseech you, hear us.*
That you grant eternal blessings
to all our family members,
relatives, and loved ones,   *we beseech you, hear us.*
That you grant eternal rest to
all the faithful departed,   *we beseech you, hear us.*
Jesus Christ, Son of God,   *we beseech you, hear us.*

Lamb of God, you take away the sins of the world,
spare us, O Lord.

Lamb of God, you take away the sins of the world,
graciously hear us, O Lord.

Lamb of God, you take away the sins of the world,
have mercy on us.

Let us pray.

Almighty, everlasting God, hear the prayers of
your Church, and in your mercy grant our petitions,
through your Son, our Lord Jesus Christ, who lives
and reigns with you in the unity of the Holy Spirit,
one God forever and ever. Amen.

PRAYERS OF
THE SAINTS

Evening Prayer

Jesus Christ, my God, I adore you and thank you for all the graces you have given me this day. I offer you my sleep and all the moments of this night, and I ask you to keep me from sin. I put myself under the protection of our Lady's mantle. Let your angels stand about me and keep me in peace. And let your blessing be upon me. Amen.

Saint Alphonsus Liguori

O God, Let Me Know You

My God, let me know and love you, so that I may find my happiness in you.

Enable me to know you ever more on earth, so that I may know you perfectly in heaven.

Enable me to love you ever more on earth, so that I may love you perfectly in heaven.

And may my joy be great on earth and perfect with you in heaven.

Saint Augustine

O God of Truth

O God of truth, grant me the happiness of heaven so that, according to your promise, my joy may be full. Until then, let my mind dwell on that happiness, my tongue speak of it, my heart long for it, my mouth proclaim it, my soul hunger for it, my flesh thirst for it, and my entire being desire it until I enter through death into the joy of my Lord forever. Amen.

Saint Augustine

For Those Awake This Night

O Lord, watch over those who are awake this
    night,
and give your angels and saints charge over those
    who sleep.
Tend your sick ones, O Lord Christ.
Give rest to your weary ones,
bless your dying ones.
Provide comfort for your suffering ones
    and compassion for your afflicted ones.
Protect your joyous ones.
All of this because you love us. Amen.

Saint Augustine

Gracious Father

Gracious and holy Father, please give me:
intellect to understand you; reason to discern
you;
diligence to seek you; wisdom to find you;
a spirit to know you; a heart to meditate upon
you;
ears to hear you; eyes to see you;
a tongue to proclaim you; a way of life pleasing
to you;
patience to wait for you; and perseverance to
look for you.
Grant me a perfect end, your holy presence,
a blessed resurrection, and life everlasting.

Saint Benedict

Lord Jesus, Forsake Us Not

Lord Jesus, who was born for us in a stable, lived for us a life of pain and sorrow, and died for us upon a cross, say for us in the hour of death, "Father, forgive," and to your Mother, "Behold your child." Say to us, "This day you shall be with me in paradise." Dear Savior, leave us not, forsake us not. We thirst for you, Fountain of Living Water. Our days pass quickly; soon all will come to an end for us. Into your hands we commend our spirits, now and forever. Amen.

Saint Elizabeth Ann Seton

The Present Moment

O Father, the first rule of our dear Savior's life
  was to do your will.
Let his will of the present moment be the first
  rule of our daily life and work,
with no other desire but for its most full and
  complete accomplishment.
Help us to follow it faithfully, so that by doing
  what you wish, we will be pleasing to you.
  Amen.

Saint Elizabeth Ann Seton

To See You Loved, O Christ

O Christ, let my greatest delight be to see you loved and your praise and glory proclaimed, especially the honor of your mercy.

O Christ, let me glorify your goodness and mercy to the last moment of my life, with every drop of my blood and every beat of my heart.

Would that I be transformed into a hymn of adoration of you.

When I find myself on my deathbed, may the last beat of my heart be a loving hymn glorifying your unfathomable mercy. Amen.

Saint Faustina

Lord, I Am Yours

Lord, I am yours, and I want to belong to no one but you.
My soul is yours, and I want to live only by you.
My will is yours, and I want to love only for you.
I want to love you as my first cause, since I am from you.
I want to love you as my final end and eternal rest, because I am for you.
I want to love you more than my own being, since my being subsists because of you.
I want to love you more than myself, because I am all yours and all in you.
Amen.

Saint Francis de Sales

My God, I Give You This Day

My God, I give you this day. I offer you, now, all the good that I do and I promise to accept, for love of you, all the difficulties I may encounter. Help me to act this day in a manner pleasing to you. Amen.

Saint Francis de Sales

God of All Glory

Great God of all glory and you, my Lord Jesus Christ, I beseech you to enlighten me and dispel the darkness of my spirit; to give me a pure faith, firm hope, and perfect charity. O my God, grant that I may come to know you better and do all things according to your light and in conformity to your most holy will. Amen.

Saint Francis of Assisi

Peace Prayer

Lord, make me an instrument of your peace.
Where there is hatred, let me sow love;
where there is injury, pardon;
where there is doubt, faith;
where there is despair, hope;

where there is darkness, light;
and where there is sadness, joy.
O Divine Master, grant that I may not so much
    seek to be consoled as to console,
to be understood as to understand,
to be loved as to love.
For it is in giving that we receive,
it is in pardoning that we are pardoned,
and it is in dying that we are born to eternal life.

Saint Francis of Assisi

Lord, Teach Me to Be Generous

Lord, teach me to be generous.
Teach me to serve you as you deserve;
to give without counting the cost;
to fight without heeding the wounds;
to toil without looking for rest;
to labor without asking for a reward
except the reward of knowing
that I am doing your holy will.

Saint Ignatius of Loyola

Prayer of Self-Offering

(Suscipe)

Take, Lord, and receive all my liberty,
my memory, my understanding, and my entire
    will—
all I have and possess.
You have given all to me.
To you, Lord, I return it.
All is yours; do with it what you will.
Give me only your love and your grace.
This is enough for me.

Saint Ignatius of Loyola

Help Me Spread Your Fragrance

Dear Jesus, help me to spread your fragrance everywhere I go. Flood my soul with your Spirit and Life. Penetrate and possess my whole being so completely that my life may only be a radiance of yours.

Shine through me, and be so in me that every person I meet may feel your presence in my soul. Let them see no longer me but only Jesus. Stay with me, and then I shall begin to shine as you shine, so to shine as to be a light to others. The light, Jesus, will

be all from you; none of it will be mine. It will be you shining on others through me. Let me praise you in the way which you love best, by shining on those around me.

Let me preach you without preaching, not by my words but by my example; by the catching force, the sympathetic influence of what I do, the evident fullness of the love my heart bears for you. Amen.

Blessed John Henry Newman

May God Give Us Peace

May God support us all the day long till the shades lengthen and the evening comes and the busy world is hushed and the fever of life is over and our work is done. Then in his mercy may God give us a safe lodging and a holy rest and peace at the last.

Blessed John Henry Newman

I Love You, My God

I love you, O my God,
and my only desire is to love you
until the last breath of my life.
I love you, O infinitely lovable God,

and I would rather die loving you
than live without loving you.
I love you, Lord,
and the only grace I ask is to love you for all
    eternity.
My God, if my tongue cannot say in every
    moment that I love you,
I want my heart to repeat it to you as often as
    I draw breath.

Saint John Vianney

O Mary, My Queen

O Mary, my Queen, I cast myself into the arms
    of your mercy.
I place my soul and body under your blessed care
    and your special protection.
I entrust to you all my hopes and consolations,
    all my anxieties and sufferings,
my entire life and the final hours of my life.
Through your most holy intercession, grant that
    all of my works may be directed and carried
    out according to your will and the will of
    your divine Son. Amen.

Saint Louis de Montfort

Christ Be with Us

May the Strength of God direct us.
May the Power of God preserve us.
May the Wisdom of God instruct us.
May the Hand of God protect us.
May the Way of God lead us.
May the Shield of God defend us.
May the Host of God guard us
against the snares of the evil ones,
against temptations of the world.
May Christ be with us!
May Christ be before us!
May Christ be in us!
Christ be over all!
May your salvation, Lord,
always be ours,
this day, O Lord, and evermore.

Saint Patrick

Lord, Be with Us Always

Christ to protect me today.
Christ with me, Christ before me, Christ behind
me, Christ in me!

Christ below me, Christ above me.
Christ at my right, Christ at my left!
Christ in breadth, Christ in length, Christ in
    height!
Christ in the heart of everyone who thinks of me,
Christ in the mouth of everyone who speaks
    to me,
Christ in every eye that sees me,
Christ in every ear that hears me!
I bind myself today to a strong virtue, an invoca-
    tion of the Trinity,
through belief in the Threeness,
through confession of the Oneness of the
    Creator of creation.
Salvation is the Lord's, salvation is the Lord's,
    salvation is Christ's.
May your salvation, O Lord, be always with us.

From the Breastplate of Saint Patrick

Day by Day

Thanks be to you, Lord Jesus Christ,
for all the blessings that you have given us,
for all the pains and insults that you have borne
    for us.

Most merciful Redeemer, Friend, and Brother,
may we know you more clearly,
love you more dearly,
and follow you more nearly,
day by day. Amen.

Saint Richard of Chichester

Christ Has No Body But Yours

Christ has no body now on earth but yours,
no hands but yours, no feet but yours.
Yours are the eyes through which
Christ's compassion looks out on the world,
yours are the feet with which
he is to go about doing good
and yours are the hands with which
he is to bless us now.
Christ has no body now on earth but yours.

Attributed to Saint Teresa of Avila

God Alone Suffices

Let nothing disturb you.
Let nothing frighten you.
All things pass away:

God never changes.
Patience obtains all things.
One who has God lacks nothing.
God alone suffices.

Saint Teresa of Avila

For Those Whom I Hold Dear

O my God! I ask you, for myself and for those whom I hold dear, the grace to fulfill perfectly your holy will, and to accept for love of you the joys and sorrows of this passing life, so that we may one day be united together in heaven for all eternity. Amen.

Saint Thérèse of Lisieux

A Student's Prayer

Divine Creator, you are the true source of life and wisdom, the One on which all else is dependent. Pour forth a single ray of your splendor and take away the darkness of sin and ignorance that fills my mind.

Grant me keenness of understanding, acuteness of memory, method and ease in learning, discernment of what I read, and rich grace with words.

Grant me strength to begin my studies well, guide me along the path of progress, and bring my studies to successful completion. I ask all this through Jesus Christ, true God and true man, who lives and reigns forever and ever. Amen.

Saint Thomas Aquinas

For Right Judgment

Grant me, O merciful God, the grace to ardently desire all that is pleasing to you; to examine it prudently, to acknowledge it truthfully, and to accomplish it perfectly for the praise and glory of your name. Amen.

Saint Thomas Aquinas

For Understanding and Wisdom

Grant me, O Lord my God, an understanding that knows you, wisdom in finding you, a way of life that is pleasing to you, perseverance that faithfully waits for you, and confidence that I shall embrace you at last.

Saint Thomas Aquinas

For Faith, Hope, and Charity

O Lord, give us a mind that is humble, quiet, peaceable, patient, and charitable, and a taste of your Holy Spirit in all our thoughts, words, and deeds.

O Lord, give us a lively faith, a firm hope, a fervent charity, a love of you.

Take from us all tepidity in meditation and all dullness in prayer.

Give us fervor and delight in thinking of you, your grace, and your tender compassion toward us.

Give us, good Lord, the grace to work for the things we pray for.

Saint Thomas More

For a Good Death

Good Lord, give me the grace to spend my life, that when the day of my death shall come, though I feel pain in my body, I may feel comfort in my soul; and with faithful hope of your mercy, in due love toward you and charity toward the world, I may, through your grace, part then into your glory.

Saint Thomas More

VARIOUS

PRAYERS

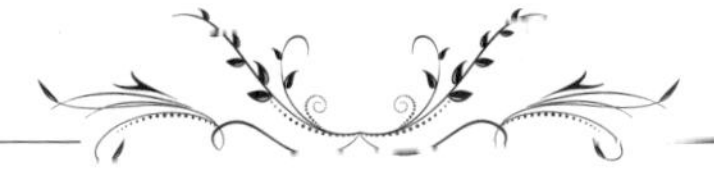

For the Dying

Merciful Father, with the death of Christ you opened the gateway to eternal life. Look kindly on all those who are close to death, especially [*name*]. United to the passion and death of your Son, and saved by the blood he shed for us, may [*name*] come before you with confidence, through Christ our Lord. Amen.

O Saint Joseph, foster father of Jesus Christ and true spouse of the Virgin Mary, pray for us and for the dying of this day.

For the Faithful Departed

My Jesus, by your sufferings during your agony in the garden, your scourging and crowning with thorns, your journey to Calvary, your crucifixion and death, have mercy on the souls of the faithful departed, especially on those who have no one to pray for them. Deliver them from their suffering and admit them to your tender embrace in heaven.

Our Father, Hail Mary, Eternal Rest . . .

O God, Creator and Redeemer of all men and women, grant to all departed souls the remission of their sins. With heartfelt prayer I ask that you grant them the pardon for their sins they so greatly desire.

Our Father, Hail Mary, Eternal Rest . . .

May my prayer, Lord, help the souls of the faithful departed, that you may free them from their sins and make them sharers in your redemption.

Our Father, Hail Mary, Eternal Rest . . .

Eternal rest grant to them, O Lord, and let perpetual light shine upon them. May they rest in peace. Amen.

May the angels lead you into paradise.
May the martyrs receive you and lead you into
   Jerusalem, the holy city of God.
May the choirs of angels receive you, and with
   Lazarus, who once was so poor, may you find
   eternal rest.

For Departed Relatives and Friends

O Jesus, good Master, I beseech you on behalf of my departed relatives and friends, especially those to whom I owe a debt of gratitude and love: parents, spouse, children, brothers, and sisters. I recommend to

you especially [*mention the name*] and also those souls who have been forgotten by their friends and family members. Admit them soon into eternal happiness.

Blessed James Alberione

For Vocations in the Church

Lord Jesus Christ, strength of those who leave all things to follow you, we pray that you raise up vocations for your Church. The harvest is great but laborers are few; send forth laborers into your harvest.

Inspire young people to understand the happiness that comes with service to others. Inspire parents to encourage their children to follow you more closely through the priesthood and religious life, and to carry on educational, charitable, and apostolic works for your Church.

Give us, Lord, fervent and apostolic priests, dedicated and self-sacrificing religious brothers and sisters. Bless your Church with priests and religious who are the salt of the earth and light for the world; who are willing to spend their lives for the glorification of your heavenly Father and the salvation of all men and women. Amen.

Blessed James Alberione

For the Choice of a Life Vocation

Heavenly Father, I believe in your wisdom and love. I believe you created me for heaven and marked out for me the path to reach it. I believe that you await me there in heaven to give me the reward of the faithful servant. Give me light and show me the pathway you want me to follow. Grant me the courage and strength to follow my life's path with peace and generosity. I ask this of you, through Jesus Christ your Son, and through Mary, my Queen and Mother. Amen.

Blessed James Alberione

For the Pope

Lord, protect from all harm our Holy Father the Pope; be his light, his strength, his consolation.

O God, Shepherd and Ruler of all your faithful people, look with mercy upon your servant Pope (*Name*), whom you have chosen to preside over your Church. Grant that he may lead your faithful by word and example, so that he may gain everlasting life together with the flock committed to him. Through Christ, your Son, our Lord. Amen.

Prayer of Those Who Live Alone

I live alone, dear Lord, stay by my side;
in all my daily needs be my guide.
Grant me good health, for that indeed I pray,
to carry on my work from day to day.
Keep pure my mind, my thoughts, my every deed;
let me be kind, unselfish in my neighbor's need.
Spare me from fire, from flood, from malicious
    tongues,
from thieves, from fear and evil ones.
If sickness or an accident befall,
then humbly, Lord, I pray, hear my call.
And when I'm feeling low, or in despair,
lift up my heart and help me in my prayer.
I live alone, dear Lord, yet have no fear,
because I feel your presence ever near. Amen.

Prayer for Families

Lead in truth, O Christ, the fathers and mothers of families. May they be urged on and strengthened by the sacramental grace of marriage and aware of being on earth the visible sign of your unfailing love for the Church. Let them be serene and firm in shouldering the responsibilities of married life and of the Christian upbringing of their children.

Lead young people in truth, O Christ. Let them not be drawn in by the idols of exaggerated consumerism, prosperity at the expense of others, moral permissiveness, and protest expressed through violence. Instead may they live with joy your message, which is the message of the Beatitudes, the message of love for God and one's neighbor, the message of moral commitment for the real transformation of society.

Lead all the faithful in truth, O Christ. May Christian faith animate their whole life and make them become, before the world, courageous witnesses of your mission of salvation. May they be responsible and dynamic members of the Church, happy sons and daughters of God, and brothers and sisters with you and with all people. Amen.

Saint John Paul II

Prayer for Veterans

Lord, God of love and mercy, bless the veterans who served our nation with courage and selfless devotion. Because of their bravery, our freedoms are upheld and our heritage preserved.

Grant them your blessings of peace and happiness in this life for the hardships they endured and the sacrifices they made to achieve victory over

tyranny and oppression. May they experience the gratitude, respect, and support from us who continue to benefit from their dedication and service.

Look with kindness, Lord, upon all departed veterans who have given their lives in the service of their country. Grant that they may share in the joy of your kingdom and rejoice with the angels and saints in heaven. We ask all this in Jesus' name. Amen.

Prayer for an Increase of Love

Jesus Master, fill my heart with love that is patient, not troubled over the shortcomings of others.

Grant me a love that is kind and thoughtful, that seeks to do good for others; a love that is not jealous but rejoices when others succeed.

Teach my heart a love that is attentive, alert, and prudent; that acts with simplicity and sincerity; that is not ambitious or intolerant, difficult to satisfy; that is not selfish but truly seeks the interests of God and my neighbor.

Master, give me a love that is humble and gentle; a love that rejoices in the truth and is happy when others are valued and appreciated.

Fill my heart with a love that can adapt to all circumstances, accepting what God permits; a love that

believes and hopes in everything, in all the good things said about others.

Jesus Master, may I be an instrument of your love.

Venerable Mother Thecla Merlo

Prayer of Thanksgiving

We give you thanks for all your benefits, O almighty God, you who live and reign forever and ever. Amen.

Thanksgiving After Receiving Holy Communion

Jesus, Truth

I adore you present in me, Incarnate Word, only begotten Son and splendor of the Father, born of Mary. I thank you, my only Master, Jesus Truth, for humbling yourself to come to me, limited and sinful as I am. With Mary I offer you to the Father: through you, with you, and in you may the Father be eternally praised and thanked. May he grant peace to all men and women. Enlighten my mind. Help me to be an authentic disciple of the Church and to live the faith I profess. Give me an understanding of the Scriptures

Make me your ardent apostle. Let the light of the Gospel, Divine Master, radiate to the farthest bounds of the world.

Jesus, Way

Jesus, you are the Way for me to follow, the perfect Model for me to imitate. In presenting myself at the judgment, I want to be found similar to you.

Divine Model of meekness and obedience, make me similar to you.

You are the perfect example of chastity and purity; make me similar to you.

You are the perfect example of love and devotion; make me similar to you.

Jesus, humble and patient, make me similar to you.

Jesus, Life

Jesus, my Life, my joy and source of all that is good, I love you. Above all, I ask that I may love you more and more and all humankind redeemed by your blood.

You are the vine and I am the branch. I want to stay united to you always so as to bear much fruit.

You are the wellspring of all grace: pour out an ever greater abundance of grace to make me holy.

Give me your Holy Spirit and all the gifts the Holy Spirit imparts.

May your kingdom come through the intercession of Mary, Queen and Mother. Console and save those dear to me. Free the souls of the departed from their sufferings. Increase vocations in your Church, and sanctify all those called to apostolic ministry. Amen.

Blessed James Alberione

Prayer for Discipleship

Blessed are you, God,
the Father of our Lord Jesus Christ,
who has blessed us in Christ
with every spiritual blessing in the heavens
    (see Eph 1:3).
Through you, Father, in Christ Jesus
we have received grace and our mission
as disciples to bring peoples of all nations
to faith and obedience in his name *(see Rm 1:5).*
Make us always ready to proclaim to all
the boundless riches of Christ . . .
so that the wisdom of God might now
be made known through the Church
    (see Eph 3:8–10).

We beg you, Father, to help us
always lead lives worthy of the vocation
to which we are called:
in humility, gentleness, and patience,
bearing with one another in love,
seeking to preserve the unity of the Spirit
by the peace that binds us together
     (see Eph 4:1–3).
Glory to you, Father,
whose power working in us
can do infinitely more
than we can ask or imagine;
glory to you from generation to generation
in the Church and in Christ Jesus forever and
     ever. Amen *(see Eph 3:20–21).*

Night Litany

We plead before you, O Jesus, for all who this
night stand in most need of your merciful love and
protection.

On those plagued by temptation,	*have mercy.*
On those who have fallen into sin,	*have mercy.*
On those who are giving themselves over to pleasure-seeking and self-indulgence,	*have mercy.*

Jesus, in your mercy, *save them.*

On those who sell their bodies
for profit, *have mercy.*

On those who force others to sell
their bodies for profit, *have mercy.*

On the victims of sin, *have mercy.*

On those frequenting the haunts
of sin and corruption, *have mercy.*

Jesus, in your mercy, *save them.*

On all who walk the streets tonight:
the homeless, the hungry, the
disillusioned, those tempted to
suicide, those who suffer from
addictions, *have mercy.*

To those who are out to
aid and rescue others, *grant help and protection.*

For those who work at night: law
enforcement, firefighters, transit
workers, entertainers, Armed Forces
or security personnel, *let your presence
be with them, Jesus.*

For the sick and suffering and all
who are enduring agony of mind
and body, *comfort them, Jesus.*

For all undergoing
emergency surgery,   *strengthen them, Jesus,
and help them in
body and soul.*

For the sleepless and lonely,   *be near them.*

For those who are anxious,
worried, or who suffer
mental distress,   *calm them.*

For the mentally ill,   *keep them under
your protection.*

For those who care for
the mentally ill,   *make them kindhearted
and compassionate.*

For night nurses,   *give them patience
and understanding.*

For priests and doctors
called out this night,   *reward them.*

Jesus, in your mercy,   *deliver them.*

For those who, this night, suffer
pain and heartache over the
death of a loved one,   *visit and sustain them.*

For those who will die
this night,   *deepen their contrition
and receive their souls.*

For those whom sudden death summons
    them before your judgment,   *have mercy.*

For those who will die alone
    without the comfort of family
    or friends,   *have mercy.*

For those dying alone without
    priest or sacrament,   *have mercy.*

On those dying blind to their sins,   *have mercy.*

On the souls of unbelievers
    who are near death,   *have mercy.*

On those who are trying to turn
    to you in their last hour,   *have mercy.*

For those who are afraid to die,   *turn their
                                              anxiety into joy.*

For dying priests and religious,   *have mercy on
                                              them and receive
                                              them to yourself.*

For the faithful departed,   *grant them light
                                              and peace.*

For ourselves in our last hour,   *grant pardon for our
                                              sins, our negligence,
                                              and our ignorance.*

Jesus, in your mercy   *deliver us all.*

On behalf of those who have said no prayers today,
let us pray:
Our Father, Hail Mary.

On behalf of those who neglect to praise God and
thank him, let us pray:
Blessed be God. Blessed be his holy name.

Praise, honor, and glory be to Jesus Christ
in the Most Holy Sacrament of the Altar.

Carmelite Monastery

Unfailing Prayer for Hope

Lord Jesus, you see my entire life.
You know my thoughts and feelings.
You see how hard life can be,
how unfair it can seem at times.
In all the confusion, one thing is certain:
your love for me never changes.
I place all my hope in you.

Embrace me as I am.
Walk with me and guide me.
Let me follow where you lead.
You desire only the greatest good for me;
you are on my side.
I place all my hope in you.

Help me see how much
you want to be part of my life.
Teach me to follow you in trust.
You are God, my Savior.
I place all my hope in you.

Blessing: "May the God of hope fill me
with all joy and peace in believing,
so that I might abound in hope by
the power of the Holy Spirit" (see Rm 15:13).

A Mother's Prayer for Her Family

O Mary, our Mother, Teacher, and Queen, you know our material and spiritual needs. Enlighten, comfort, and provide for our family. In your love for us, please ensure that we will always be united in heart and soul.

We trust in you and entrust ourselves to you. With your help, we want to make our home a place of harmony and love, a place where Jesus willingly remains among us. We want to be united heart and soul with him, with you, and among ourselves. And at this life's end, we want to attain together a beautiful heaven, where we will praise and thank you for all eternity.

Venerable Mother Thecla Merlo

PRAYERS FROM SCRIPTURE

New Testament Prayers

That I May See in Faith

O God, help us to see in faith
that affliction produces steadfastness,
steadfastness produces proven character,
and proven character produces hope,
a hope that is no illusion,
because through the Holy Spirit
you have poured out your love in our hearts.

(See Rm 5:3–5)

That Christ May Dwell in My Heart

I bend my knees to you, Father,
from whom every family in the heavens and on
    earth is named.
I ask that from the riches of your glory
you may grant me inner strength and power
    through your Spirit,

so Christ may dwell in my heart through faith.
With all the saints may I be able to understand
the breadth, the length, the height, and the
    depth of Christ's love;
and knowing Christ's love, which surpasses all
    knowledge,
may I be filled with all God's fullness.
To you, O God,
who are able to do so much more than I can ask
    for or imagine,
by your power at work in me,
be glory in the Church in Christ Jesus for all
    generations,
forever and ever. Amen.

(See Eph 3:14–21)

That We May Be Worthy

Make us worthy, Lord God,
of the life that you have called us to live.
By your power fulfill in us every desire for
    goodness
and every work of faith, so that through us
    the name
of our Lord Jesus Christ will be glorified.

(See 2 Th 1:11–12)

That I May Not Worry

Lord Jesus,
grant that I may not worry too much about
my life—what I will eat or what I will drink—
or about my body—what I will wear.
Help me to understand
that life is more than food,
and the body more than clothing.
Increase my faith in my heavenly Father
who knows all my needs.
Increase my faith that by first seeking
God's kingdom and his will,
all these things will be given to me as well.

(See Mt 6:25, 32–33)

Grant Me Peace

Lord, grant me your peace, which is beyond all
    understanding
and which will keep my heart and mind in
    Christ Jesus.
Fill my heart and thoughts with all that is true,
honorable, just, pure, pleasing, gracious,
virtuous, and praiseworthy.

Grant me your peace, O Lord, and may it remain
with me always.

(See Ph 4:7–9)

All Glory Be to God

O God, how immense is your richness, wisdom,
and knowledge!
How unfathomable are your judgments, how
inscrutable your ways!
For who can know your mind, O Lord?
Who could ever be your counselor?
Who could ever be the giver and you the One to
repay the gift?
For all things are from you, through you, and in
you.
To you, O God, be glory forever. Amen.

(See Rm 11:33–36)

Lord, You Are Holy

Great and awesome are your works,
Lord God almighty!
Just and true are your ways,

King of all nations!
Is there anyone who does not fear you, Lord,
or glorify your name?
Because you alone are holy;
all nations will come
and worship before you,
for your just judgments have been revealed.

(See Rv 15:3–4)

Lord, You Freed Us From Sin

Grace and peace from the One who is,
who was, and who is to come,
from the seven spirits before his throne,
and from Jesus Christ, the faithful witness
—the firstborn from the dead.
He loves us and has freed us from our sins,
and has made us a kingdom,
priests to his God and Father.
To him be glory and power forever. Amen.

(See Rv 1:4–6)

Psalms

Trust in God

(Psalm 62)

My soul, silently trust in God alone,
    for it is from him that I draw my hope.
He alone is my rock, my stronghold and my
        salvation
    —my fortress. I shall not waver.
My salvation and glory rest in God;
    the stronghold that protects me
    and my sanctuary is in God.
Trust in him, you people, whatever the times.
    Pour out your hearts in the presence of the
        Lord.
    God is a refuge for us.
Yours, O Lord, is loving kindness;
    for you repay every person
    according to their deeds.

The Lord Abides with Us

(Psalm 23)

The LORD is my shepherd;
    nothing do I want.
He makes me lie down in verdant pastures,
    he guides me along soothing streams.
He refreshes my soul.
    He leads me along paths of righteousness
    for the sake of his name.
Even though I walk in the dark valley I fear
        no evil,
    because you are with me.
    Your rod and your staff give me courage.
You spread the table before me in the face of
        my foes;
    you have anointed my head with oil;
    my cup overflows.
May only contentment and loving kindness
    be with me all the days of my life,
    and may I dwell in the house of the LORD
        for years to come.

In Praise of God's Faithfulness

(Psalm 92)

> It is good to give thanks to the Lord,
>> to sing psalms to your name, Most High;
> to declare your loving kindness in the morning
>> and your faithfulness every night,
> with the sound of a ten-stringed lyre,
>> and the music of a harp.
> For you, Lord, have made me rejoice because
>> of your works;
>> I shout for joy at the works of your hands.
> How great, O Lord, are your deeds,
>> how deep your designs.

May God Bless Us

(Psalm 67)

> O God, be gracious to us and bless us.
>> Let your face shine upon us,
> that your way may be known on earth
>> and your salvation, among all nations.
> Let the peoples praise you, O God,
>> let all the peoples praise you.

Let the nations sing and shout with joy,
> for you judge the peoples with righteousness
> and guide the nations on the earth.
Let the peoples praise you, O God,
> let all the peoples praise you.
The earth has brought forth its fruit.
> May God, our God, bless us.
May God indeed bless us,
> and may all the ends of the earth revere him.

Trust in God's Mercy

(Psalm 103)

Bless the LORD, my soul;
> all my being, bless his holy name.
Bless the LORD, my soul,
> and let not all his kindnesses be forgotten:
he forgives all your guilt;
> he heals all your infirmities;
he rescues your life from the grave;
> he crowns you with loving kindness and
> > tender love;
he bestows fulfilling goodness upon your years.
The LORD is compassionate and gracious,
> slow to anger and rich in loving kindness.

Rely on the Lord

(Psalm 25)

> To you, O LORD, I lift up my soul.
> In you, my God, I trust;
>   I shall not be disappointed.
> Indeed, those who rely on you shall not be
>   disappointed.
> Give me knowledge of your ways, O LORD;
>   instruct me in your paths.
> Make me walk in your truth and teach me.
>   Because you are my saving God,
>   it is on you that I have relied at all times.

In Praise of God's Mercy

(Psalm 113)

> Praise, you servants of the LORD,
>   praise the name of the LORD.
> May the name of the LORD be blessed,
>   now and forevermore.
> The name of the LORD is to be praised
>   from the rising of the sun to its setting.
> The LORD is exalted over all the nations,
>   his splendor is above the heavens.

Who is like the Lord our God,
who is enthroned on high,
who deigns to look down upon heaven and
earth?
The Lord raises the poor from the dust,
lifts up the needy from the ash heap,
to give them a place among the princes,
among the rulers of his people.

SEASONAL PRAYERS

Advent

The word "advent" originates from the Latin and means "coming" or "arrival." It marks the beginning of a new Church year, a time of hope and anticipation. During this season we prepare not only for the annual feast of Jesus' birth, but we contemplate his second coming, watching for the day when Christ will come again in glory.

Come, O Lord!

Let the heavens be glad and the earth rejoice.
O all you mountains, praise the Lord.
Drop down dew from above, you heavens,
and let the clouds rain the Just One.
Let the earth be opened
and bud forth the Savior.
Remember us, O Lord,
and visit us in your salvation.
Show your mercy to us, O Lord,

and grant us your salvation.
Send forth, O Lord, the Lamb, the Ruler of
    the earth,
from the rock in the desert to the mount
    of Sion.
Come to free us, O Lord, God of hosts;
show your face, and we shall be saved.
Come, O Lord, and visit us in peace,
so that we may rejoice before you with a perfect
    heart.
May we know on earth, O Lord, your way,
your salvation among all nations.
Put forth, O Lord, your strength,
and come to save us.
Come, O Lord, and do not hesitate;
pardon the sins of your people.
O, that you would rend the heavens and come
    down,
the mountains would melt in your presence.
Come, and show us your face, O Lord,
you who sit upon the cherubim.

Compiled from Old Testament Scripture

With Longing for the Lord's Coming

Father in heaven,
our hearts desire the warmth of your love
and our minds are searching for the light of your
    Word.
Increase our longing for Christ our Savior
and give us the strength to grow in love,
that the dawn of his coming
may find us rejoicing in his presence
and welcoming the light of his truth.
We ask this in the name of Jesus the Lord.
    Amen.

Roman Missal, 2nd Edition

Prayer of Praise

All praise and thanks to you, O God,
for through your tender mercy,
Jesus, the shining Light from on high,
    will visit us.
He will give light to those in darkness and
in the shadow of death.
He will guide our steps along the way of peace.
Come, Lord Jesus!

(See Luke 1:78–79; Rv 22:20)

CHRISTMAS

Emmanuel, God is with us. At Christmas we celebrate the wonder of the Incarnation. Jesus Christ, the Word made flesh for our salvation, is born in time. We recall Jesus' humble birth and the awesome mystery of God's love for humankind. The child held in the arms of Mary is our God made visible.

Prayer to Obtain Favors

Hail and blessed be the hour and the moment in which the Son of God was born of the Most Holy Virgin Mary at midnight, in Bethlehem, in piercing cold. In that hour, O God, I ask that you hear my prayer and grant my request through the merits of our Savior Jesus Christ and his blessed Mother. Amen.

Traditionally this prayer is recited daily from November 30, the feast of Saint Andrew, until December 24, Christmas Eve

A Song of Praise

Sing a new song to the Lord,
sing to the Lord, all the earth!
Sing to the Lord, bless his name.
Proclaim the good news of his salvation, day
after day.
Speak of his glory among the nations,
his wonders among all the peoples.

Let the heavens rejoice and the earth be glad;
let the sea, and all that is in it, resound.
Let the countryside, and all that is in it, exult.
Then shall all the trees in the forest shout for joy
at the presence of the Lord for he comes,
for he comes to mete out justice on the earth.
He will judge the world with righteousness,
and the peoples with his faithfulness.

(See Psalm 96)

Prayer to the Infant Jesus

Jesus, Word of the Father, Son of God, you assumed a human nature in order to accomplish our salvation. You are Lord of heaven and earth, yet, born of the Virgin Mary, you chose to come to us as an infant, unpretentious and wholly dependent on others for your needs. Your example of littleness, simplicity, and spontaneous trust awakens in my heart a great desire to follow the path of spiritual childhood. Infant Lord, teach me to love humility and to understand that what is small and insignificant in the eyes of the world is most often the foundation for greatness in your kingdom. Lead me along the path of childlike gentleness and availability. Grant that I may welcome each new day with childlike expectancy, and grant me a renewed portion of the energy and vitality of a child, that I may serve the needs of others and in so doing serve you, my Lord and God. Amen.

The Father's Love

Heavenly Father, you have shown us how great your love is for us by sending your only-begotten Son into the world, that we might have life and the forgiveness of our sins through him. If you, Lord, loved us so much, we too should love one another. Teach us how to love others. Remain in us, so that your love is made perfect in us. Amen.

(See 1 Jn 4:9–12)

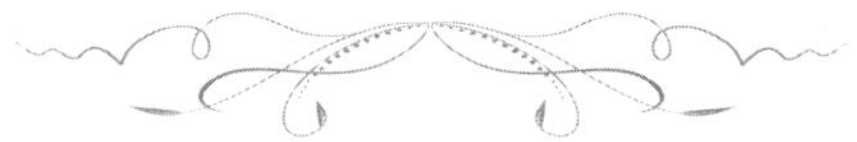

LENT

Lent is the forty days of preparation for Easter. Through prayer, fasting, and almsgiving, the Church invites us to share more intensely in the mystery of Christ's saving death and resurrection.

Prayer Before a Crucifix

Good and gentle Jesus, I kneel before you and with fervent desire ask that you fill my heart with sentiments of faith, hope, and love, repentance for my sins, and true conversion of life.

As I see and contemplate your five precious wounds, I recall the words that David prophesied long ago, my Jesus: "They have pierced my hands and my feet; they have counted all my bones" *(Ps 22:17–18)*.

To Live a Holy Life

With your grace, Lord, help us
to renounce ungodly living
and worldly passions,
and to live temperate, upright,
and godly lives in this present age
as we await our blessed hope—
the appearance in glory of our great God
and Savior, Jesus Christ. Amen.

(See Tt 2:12–13)

A Prayer for Forgiveness

From the depths I call to you, O Lord.
Lord, listen to my voice.
Let your ears be attentive
    to my voice in supplication.
If you, O Lord, keep an account of sins,
    Lord, who can stand?
But with you is forgiveness,
    for this we revere you.
I wait for the Lord,
    my soul depends on his word.
My soul waits for the Lord
    more than watchmen for the dawn,

Yes, more than watchmen wait for the dawn.
Israel, depend on the LORD,
    for with the LORD is loving kindness
    and fullness of redemption.
And he will redeem Israel
    from all its iniquities.

(Psalm 130)

The Way of the Cross

Christians of every age have desired to walk in the footsteps of Jesus and accompany him along the *Via Dolorosa*. Pilgrims of the early centuries were actually able to travel to the Holy Land and walk the road to Calvary. It is said that Mary, the Mother of Jesus, was the first to revisit these sacred places. But it was only in the fourth century that the first accounts were written describing the veneration of certain places in Jerusalem where shrines had been erected by the Roman Emperor Constantine.

As the centuries passed, replicas of these shrines appeared in various places and could be found throughout Europe. These carvings in stone or wood, and the pictorial representations of the Jerusalem shrines, were intended to help Christians recall the events of Jesus' passion.

Today, we see fourteen similar representations in our churches; the number and sequence of these stations was established by Pope Clement XII in 1731.

Devotion to the passion of Christ through the Stations of the Cross was promoted especially by the Franciscans, who were largely responsible for developing and placing artistic representations in churches throughout the Western world. It is said that Leonard of Port Maurice, who is known for his efforts to popularize this devotion, erected over five hundred sets of stations within twenty years; the best known among them is located in the Coliseum at Rome.

A plenary indulgence is granted the Christian faithful who devoutly pray the Way of the Cross, uniting their own sufferings to those of Jesus.

Opening Prayer

O Father, who has loved us to the point of sacrificing your most beloved Son, fill us with your Holy Spirit. May he make us true disciples of Christ, who are filled with the wisdom of the cross and joyful in the hope of eternal salvation. Through the same Christ, our Lord. Amen.

First Station

The most innocent Jesus accepts, for the glory of God and peace to all peoples, the unjust sentence of death pronounced against him by Pilate.

℣. We adore you, O Christ, and we bless you.
℟. Because by your holy cross you have
redeemed the world.

"Pilate said to them, 'Then what should I do
with Jesus, who is called the Messiah?'
They all said, 'Let him be crucified!'
'But what wrong has he done?' he asked.
But they shouted all the more and said, 'Let him
be crucified!'

Then he released Barabbas to them, but he had
Jesus scourged and handed him over to be
crucified" (Mt 27:22–23, 26).

O Jesus, may your will and not mine be done in all things.

Stabat Mater

At the cross her station keeping
Stood the mournful mother weeping,
Close to Jesus to the last.

Second Station

Jesus takes the cross upon his shoulders. Jesus our Master invites us: "Whoever wishes to come after me must deny themselves, take up their cross, and follow me."

℣. We adore you, O Christ, and we bless you.
℟. Because by your holy cross you have
　　redeemed the world.

"Then the governor's soldiers took Jesus along to the praetorium and gathered the whole cohort around him. They stripped him and put a scarlet robe on him, and after weaving a crown of thorns they put it on his head and placed a reed in his right hand, and they knelt before him and mocked him, saying, 'Hail, King of the Jews!' And after spitting on him they took the reed and beat him over the head. And when they were done mocking him they stripped the robe off him and dressed him in his own clothes and led him off to be crucified" (Mt 27:27–31).

O Jesus, by my guide and my comfort on my journey through life.

Through her heart his sorrow sharing,
All his bitter anguish bearing,
Now at length the sword had passed.

THIRD STATION

Wearied by the agony in Gethsemane, tortured by the scourging and the crowning with thorns, exhausted by fasting, Jesus falls for the first time beneath the massive weight of the cross.

℣. We adore you, O Christ, and we bless you.
℟. Because by your holy cross you have
    redeemed the world.

"Surely he has borne our infirmities
and carried our diseases;
yet we accounted him stricken,
struck down by God, and afflicted.
But he was wounded for our transgressions,
crushed for our iniquities;
upon him was the punishment that made us
    whole,
and by his bruises we are healed.

All we like sheep have gone astray;
we have all turned to our own way;
and the Lord has laid on him
the iniquity of us all" (Is 53:4–6).

O Jesus, give me strength in temptation and deliver me from all evil.

Stabat Mater

Oh, how sad and sore distressed
Was that mother highly blest
Of the sole-begotten one!

FOURTH STATION

Carrying the cross, Jesus meets his mother, whose soul is struck by a sword of sorrow. The hearts of Jesus and Mary are united in the same suffering.

℣. We adore you, O Christ, and we bless you.
℟. Because by your holy cross you have
      redeemed the world.

"And Simeon blessed them and said to his mother, Mary, 'Behold, he is destined to bring about the fall and rise of many in Israel, and to be a sign that will be opposed, and a sword shall pierce your own soul' . . . His mother kept all these things in her heart" (Lk 2:34–35, 51).

O Jesus, grant me the grace to better know, love, and imitate you.

Stabat Mater

Christ above in torment hangs,
She beneath beholds the pangs
Of her dying, glorious Son.

FIFTH STATION

Simon of Cyrene is coerced by the soldiers to help carry the cross of Jesus.

℣. We adore you, O Christ, and we bless you.
℟. Because by your holy cross you have
　　redeemed the world.

"As they were going out they found a man named Simon of Cyrene; they forced this man to carry the cross of Jesus" (Mt 27:32).

O Jesus, grant that I may follow you even along the road of suffering.

Is there one who would not weep,
Whelmed in miseries so deep,
Christ's dear mother to behold?

SIXTH STATION

With heartfelt compassion, Veronica wipes the bloodstained face of Jesus, and Jesus rewards her by leaving the impression of his face on the towel.

℣. We adore you, O Christ, and we bless you.
℟. Because by your holy cross you have
    redeemed the world.

"He had no form or majesty that we should look
    at him,
nothing in his appearance that we should desire
    him.
He was despised and rejected by others;
a man of suffering and acquainted with
    infirmity;
and as one from whom others hide their
    faces. . ." (Is 53:2–3).

*O Jesus, lovable face of the Suffering Servant disfig-
ured by our sins, have mercy on us.*

Stabat Mater

> Can the human heart refrain
> From partaking in her pain,
> In that mother's pain untold?

SEVENTH STATION

Jesus' strength fails, and he who was made the
"scorn of men" and the "rejected one of the people"
falls a second time beneath the cross.

℣. We adore you, O Christ, and we bless you.
℟. Because by your holy cross you have
   redeemed the world.

"I am a man who has seen affliction under the
   rod of God's wrath;
he has driven and brought me into darkness
   without any light; . . .
he has blocked my ways with hewn stones,
he has made my paths crooked. . . .
He has made my teeth grind on gravel, and
   made me cower in ashes" (Lam 3:1–2, 9, 16).

"For our high priest is not one who is unable to sympathize with our weaknesses; he was tempted in every way we are, yet never sinned" (Heb 4:15).

O Jesus, when I fall under the weight of temptation, lift me up again.

Stabat Mater

Bruised, derided, cursed, defiled,
She beheld her tender child,
All with bloody scourges rent.

EIGHTH STATION

The "daughters of Jerusalem" come to meet Jesus, weeping and lamenting in profound grief as mothers grieving with their children during a tragic hour in their history.

℣. We adore you, O Christ, and we bless you.
℟. Because by your holy cross you have
    redeemed the world.

"Now a large crowd of the people was following him, as well as women who were lamenting and wailing for him. But Jesus turned to them and said, 'Daughters of Jerusalem, do not weep for me; weep,

instead, for yourselves and for your children'" (Lk 23:27–29).

O Jesus, save me by the grace of your redeeming love.

Stabat Mater

Let me share with you his pain,
Who for all my sins was slain,
Who for me in torment died.

NINTH STATION

Jesus falls the third time beneath the cross to touch the heart of each person who stumbles beneath the weight of unyielding trials.

℣. We adore you, O Christ, and we bless you.
℟. Because by your holy cross you have
     redeemed the world.

"Come to me, all you grown weary and burdened, and I will refresh you.

"Take my yoke upon you and learn from me, for I am gentle and humble hearted" (Mt 11:28–29).

O Jesus, set me free from the yoke of sin; pardon my offenses.

> O my Mother, fount of love,
> Touch my spirit from above;
> Make my heart with yours accord.

TENTH STATION

Having reached Calvary, Jesus is stripped of his garments and given a bitter mixture of gall and myrrh to drink.

℣. We adore you, O Christ, and we bless you.

℟. Because by your holy cross you have
redeemed the world.

"When the soldiers had crucified Jesus they took his cloak and made four parts, one for each soldier, plus the tunic. Now the tunic was seamless, woven from the top in one piece. So they said to each other, 'Let's not tear it; let's draw lots for it instead,' so the Scripture would be fulfilled which said, 'They divided my garments among them, and for my clothing they cast lots'" (Jn 19:23–24).

O Jesus, clothe me with the garments of holiness and forgiveness.

Make me feel as you have felt,
Make my soul to glow and melt
With the love of Christ my Lord.

Eleventh Station

The executioners nail Jesus to the cross beneath the gaze of his most sorrowful mother, causing him unspeakable agony.

℣. We adore you, O Christ, and we bless you.
℟. Because by your holy cross you have
redeemed the world.

"After crucifying him . . . they sat down and kept watch over him there. And over his head they placed the written charge against him, 'This is Jesus the King of the Jews.' Then two robbers were crucified with him, one on his right and one on his left. The passersby kept blaspheming him, shaking their heads and saying, 'If you are the Son of God, come down from the cross!' The chief priests along with the scribes and elders also mocked him, saying, 'He saved others but cannot save himself! If he is the

King of Israel, let him come down now from the cross and we will believe in him'" (Mt 27:35–42).

O Jesus, I want to belong to you in life, in death, and in eternity. Do not let me separate myself from you.

Stabat Mater

Holy Mother, pierce me through,
In my heart each wound renew
Of my Savior crucified.

TWELFTH STATION

Jesus suffers for three hours, then dies on the cross for our sins.

℣. We adore you, O Christ, and we bless you.
℟. Because by your holy cross you have
    redeemed the world.

"Now from about noon darkness came upon the land until about three o'clock. Then at about three Jesus cried out with a loud voice and said, *'Eli, Eli, lema sabachthani?'* that is, 'My God, my God, why have you forsaken me?' . . . Jesus cried out again in a loud voice and gave up the spirit" (Mt 27:45–50).

O Jesus, Lamb of God who takes away the sins of the world, have mercy on us.

Stabat Mater

For the sins of his own nation
She saw him hang in desolation
Till his spirit forth he sent.

THIRTEENTH STATION

Mary, filled with sorrow, receives her Son into her arms after he had been taken down from the cross.

℣. We adore you, O Christ, and we bless you.
℟. Because by your holy cross you have
   redeemed the world.

"There were many women there, watching from a distance, who had followed Jesus from Galilee to serve him. . . . When evening had come a rich man from Arimathea named Joseph, who had also been a disciple of Jesus, came; he went to Pilate and requested the body of Jesus. Then Pilate ordered it to be given to him" (Mt 27:55–58)

O Mary, accept me as your child. Accompany me throughout my life; be with me daily, especially in the hour of my death.

Stabat Mater

Let me mingle tears with you,
Mourning him who mourned for me
All the days that I may live.

FOURTEENTH STATION

The body of Jesus, anointed with spices, is brought to the sepulcher. With strong faith, Mary, his mother, awaits the resurrection of her Son, as he foretold.

℣. We adore you, O Christ, and we bless you.
℟. Because by your holy cross you have
   redeemed the world.

"Joseph took the body and wrapped it in a clean linen shroud and placed it in his new tomb, which he had hewn in the rock, and after rolling a large stone up to the door of the tomb he went away. Now Mary Magdalen and the other Mary were there, sitting across from the sepulcher" (Mt 27:59–61).

O Jesus, my Life and Resurrection, I believe in you; I hope in you; I love you.

Stabat Mater

While my body here decays,
May my soul your goodness praise,
Safe in paradise with you. Amen.

CLOSING PRAYER

Father, you have willed to save men and women through the death of Christ your Son on the cross. Grant that we who have known his mystery of love on earth may enjoy the fruits of the redemption in heaven. We ask this through Christ our Lord. Amen.

In conclusion, pray one Our Father, one Hail Mary, and one Glory to the Father for the intentions of the Holy Father.

Based on the Way of the Cross
by Blessed James Alberione

Easter

Easter is the season of the glorious "Alleluia!" It is the season of promise. Christ has triumphed; he has broken the power of death. His victory over death is our victory.

A Hymn of Praise to the Risen Christ
(*Victimae Paschali Laudes*)

Christians, to the Paschal Victim
offer your thankful praises!
A lamb the sheep redeems: Christ,
who only is sinless,
reconciles sinners to the Father.
Death and life have contended in that combat
    stupendous:
the prince of life, who died, reigns immortal.
Speak, Mary, declaring
what you saw, wayfaring.
"The tomb of Christ, who is living,

the glory of Jesus' resurrection;
bright angels attesting,
the shroud and napkin resting.
Yes, Christ my hope is arisen:
to Galilee he goes before you."
Christ indeed from death is risen, our new life
    obtaining.
Have mercy, victor King, ever reigning!
Amen. Alleluia.

Praise the Lord

Everything that lives and breathes, praise the LORD.

Alleluia.
Praise God in his sanctuary,
    praise him in his mighty firmament.
Praise him for his powerful deeds,
    praise his immense greatness.
Praise him to the blast of trumpets,
    praise him to the sound of lyre and harp.
Praise him to the sound of tambourines and
        dance,
    praise him to the sound of strings and pipes.
Praise him to the sound of clanging cymbals,
    praise him to the sound of clashing cymbals.

Let everything that breathes praise the Lord.
Alleluia.

(Psalm 150)

To the Father of Mercies

Blessed are you, God
and Father of our Lord Jesus Christ,
our compassionate Father
and ever encouraging God.
Blessed are you, God
and Father of our Lord Jesus Christ!
In your great mercy
we have been reborn to a living hope
through the resurrection
of Jesus Christ from the dead
and to an imperishable,
undefiled, and unfading inheritance.

(See 1 Cor 1:3 and 1 Pt 1:3–4)

LATIN PRAYERS AND HYMNS

Signum Crucis

In nomine Patris, et Filii, et Spiritus Sancti. Amen.

Angelus Domini

Ángelus Dómini nuntiávit Maríæ.
Et concépit de Spíritu Sancto.
Ave, María . . .

Ecce ancílla Dómini.
Fiat mihi secúndum verbum tuum.
Ave, María . . .

Et Verbum caro factum est.
Et habitávit in nobis.
Ave, María . . .

Ora pro nobis, sancta Dei génetrix.
Ut digni efficiámur promissiónibus Christi.

Orémus.

Grátiam tuam, quæsumus,
Dómine, méntibus nostris infúnde;
ut qui, Ángelo nuntiánte,
Christi Fílii tui incarnatiónem cognóvimus,
per passiónem eius et crucem,
ad resurrectiónis glóriam perducámur.

Per eúndem Christum Dóminum nostrum.
Amen.

Glória Patri . . .

Regina Cæli

Regína cæli lætáre, allelúia.
Quia quem meruísti portáre, allelúia.
Resurréxit, sicut dixit, allelúia.
Ora pro nobis Deum, allelúia.

V. Gaude et lætáre, Virgo María, allelúia.
℟. Quia surréxit Dóminus vere, allelúia.

Orémus.

Deus, qui per resurrectiónem Fílii tui Dómini nostri Iesu Christi mundum lætificáre dignátus es, præsta, quæsumus, ut per eius Genetrícem Vírginem Maríam perpétuæ capiámus gáudia vitæ. Per Christum Dóminum nostrum. Amen.

Glória Patri . . .

Pater Noster

Pater noster, qui es in caelis, sanctificetur nomen tuum. Adveniat regnum tuum. Fiat volúntas tua,

sicut in caelo et in terra. Panen nostrum quotidiá-
num da nobis hódie. Et dimítte nobis débita nostra,
sicut et nos dimittimus debitoribus nostris. Et ne nos
inducas in tentationem, sed libera nos a malo. Amen.

Ave, Maria

Ave, Maria, grátia plena; Dóminus tecum:
benedícta tu in muliéribus, et benedíctus fructus
ventris tui, Jesus. Sancta María, Mater Dei, ora pro
nobis peccatóribus, nunc et in hora mortis nostrae.
Amen.

Gloria Patri

Glória Patri, et Fílio, et Spirítui Sancto. Sicut erat
in princípio, et nunc, et semper, et in saécula saeculórum. Amen.

Salve, Regina

Salve, Regina, mater misericórdiae; vita, dulcédo
et spes nostra, salve. Ad te clamámus, éxules filii
Evae. Ad te suspiramus geméntes et flentes in hac
lacrimárum valle. Eia ergo, advocata nostra, illos tuos

misericórdes óculos ad nos convérte. Et Jesum, benedictum fructum ventris tui, nobis, post hoc exsílium, ostende. O clemens, o pia, o dulcis Virgo Maria.

Memorare

Memorare, o piisima Virgo Maria, non esse auditum a saeculo, quemquam ad tua currentem praesidia, tua implorantem auxilia, tua petentem suffragia esse derelicta. Nos tali animati confidentia ad te, Virgo Virginum, Mater, currimus; ad te venimus; coram te gementes peccatores assistimus. Noli, Mater Verbi, verba nostra despicere, sed audi propitia et exaudi. Amen.

Angele Dei

Angele Dei, qui custos es mei, me tibi commissum pietáta supérna illumina, custodi, rege et gubérna. Amen.

Réquiem Aetérnam

Réquiem aetérnam dona eis, Dómine: et lux perpétua luceat eis. Requiéscant in pace. Amen.

Adorámus Te, Christe

Adorámus te, Christe, et benedícimus tibi. Quia per sanctam crucem et mortem tuam redemisti mundum.

Anima Christi

Anima Christi, sanctífica me;
Corpus Christi, salva me;
Sanguis Christi, inébria me;
Aqua láteris Christi, lava me;
Pássio Christi, confórta me;
O bone Jesu, exáudi me.
Intra vúlnera tua, abscónde me;
Ne permíttas me separári a te;
Ab hoste malígno defénde me;
In hora mortis meae voca me;
Et iube me venire ad te;
Ut cum sanctis tuis laudem te.
Per infinita saécula saeculórum. Amen.

Sub Tuum Praesídium

Sub tuum praesídium confúgimus,
Sancta Dei Génitrix:
Nostras deprecatiónis

Ne despícias in necessitátibus:
Sed a perículis cunctis líbera nos semper,
Virgo gloriósa et benedícta. Amen.

Agimus Tibi Gratias

Agimus tibi grátias, omnipotens Deus, pro univé-
rsis benefíciis tuis. Qui vivis et regnas in saécula saeculórum. Amen.

Magnificat

Magníficat ánima mea Dóminum.
Et exultávit spíritus meus in Deo salutári meo.
Quia respéxit humilitátem ancíllae suae
Ecce enim ex hoc beátam me dicent omnes
    generatiónes.
Quia fécit mihi mágna qui pótens est, et
    sánctum nómen eius.
Et misericórdia eius in progénies et progénies
    timéntibus eum.
Fécit poténtiam in brácchio suo; dispérsit
    supérbos mente cordis sui.
Depósuit poténtes de sede, et exaltávit húmiles.
Esuriéntes implévit bonis, et dívites dimísit
    inánes.

Suscépit Ísrael, púerum suum, recordátus
   misericórdiae suae.
Sicut locútus est ad patres nostros, Ábraham,
   et sémini eius in saecula.
Glória Patri, et Fílio, et Spirítui Sancto,
Sicut erat in princípio, et nunc, et semper, et in
   sæcula sæculórum. Amen.

O Salutáris

O salutáris hóstia,
Quae caeli pandis óstium.
Bella premunt hostília,
Da robur fer auxílium.
Uni Trinóque Domino
Sit sempitérna glória,
Qui vitam sine término
Nobis donet in patria. Amen.

Tantum Ergo

Tantum ergo sacraméntum
Venerémur cérnui:
Et antíquum documéntum
Novo cedat rítui:
Praestet fídes suppleméntum

Sénsuum deféctui.
Genitóri, genitóque
Laus et iubilátio,
Salus, honor, virtus quoque
Sit et benedictio:
Procedénti ab utróque
Compar sit laudatio. Amen.

Panis Angelicus

Panis angelicus
Fit panis hominum;
Dat panis coelicus
Figuris terminum:
O res mirabilis!
Manducat Dominum
Pauper, servus, et humilis.

Te trina Deitas,
Unaque poscimus,
Sic nos tu visita,
Sicut te colimus;
Per tuas semitas
Duc nos quo tendimus,
Ad lucem quam inhabitas.

HELPS FOR SPIRITUAL GROWTH

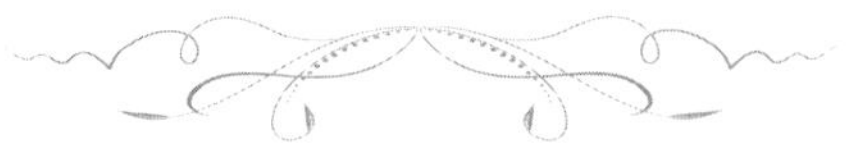

Method for a Daily Examination of Conscience

If you feel a desire to set out on the path to holiness of life, self-awareness is one of the keys to achieve that desire. Self-knowledge is an ongoing process leading to spiritual growth as one begins to listen attentively to the voice of conscience. Everyone has this inner voice at the core of their being, and here every person is truly alone with God. This voice, which speaks without words, consistently calls every person to do good and avoid evil. Attentive to this inner voice, the heart asks: How well have I been living as a follower of Jesus Christ? The candid response to this question sets one on the path to self-honesty and opens the way to holiness of life.

The practice of the daily examen (for ten or fifteen minutes) offers the opportunity to look at how things stand between yourself and God; it offers the chance to assess the dynamics of your relationship with God, giving you an opportunity to evaluate some of your priorities. God speaks in many ways, but how well are you listening? Consider using the following outline for the practice of your daily examen:

- Choose a quiet space and recollect yourself. Call upon the Holy Spirit to help you be attentive to the Lord's presence in and around you, and then wait and find comfort in God who is with you.

- As you reflect on your day, recall those experiences that bring to mind the generosity and goodness of God. Call to mind the reasons you have to be grateful. What are you most thankful for, today?

- Ask for the grace to see yourself as God, who is your Savior, sees you.

- Review the day, and converse with God about the things that happened at work, at home. Think about your interactions with co-workers and family members, etc., and identify significant thoughts, actions, omissions, and desires that speak to you about your relationship with God, with others, and with yourself. Is there something that stands out today? Is there a pattern to this kind of behavior?

✢ Speak to the Lord about those aspects and ask for insight to know what these things reveal about you and your relationship with God. Acknowledge those patterns of behavior and attitudes that disrupt your relationship with God and others, and ask the Lord for mercy, giving thanks for his unconditional love for you.

✢ Look ahead and decide how you will act tomorrow, taking steps to leave behind those thoughts or actions that diminish your resolve to live as a committed follower of Jesus Christ. Make an act of trust in God, and ask for the grace to live your life in his love.

THE SACRAMENT
OF RECONCILIATION

An important part of preparing for the sacrament of Reconciliation is an "examination of conscience." During this exercise, the penitent sets time aside to think and to pray. The main question to ask ourselves is: How well have I been living as a disciple of Jesus Christ, and where have I failed?

Sometimes we can answer this question immediately. There will be obvious examples of failure. Each of us has long-established patterns of weakness. We find ourselves making the same mistakes and committing the same sins repeatedly, the "old standbys" that keep us awake at night. But there are also more subtle ways in which we stray from Christ's example. Sin hides well. By looking at ourselves carefully, though, we may discover the unexpected sins in our lives. We may even be able to see patterns of sin that we did not recognize before. Clarity is the purpose of examining one's conscience. By seeing more clearly, we are better able to seek the help we need. By seeking help, we become freer in drawing closer to God.

As you prepare for Confession, ask God to help you see and accept the particular sins for which you are responsible. Then explore your behavior since your last confession. One way to jog your mind and heart is through reflection on the Ten Commandments, which is one way to help focus your thoughts and look over your life.

I am the Lord your God; you shall not have strange gods before me.

Do you let other desires interfere with knowing, loving, and serving God? Do you doubt God's love for you? Have you boasted about sinning? Have you let love of material goods, physical pleasures, or personal status determine your choices? Are you angry with God? Do you believe you do not need God? Do you pray regularly? Have you broken vows or promises made to God? Have you sought control over your life through superstition, magic, witchcraft, or those who claim to possess psychic powers? Have you prayed that harm might come to someone?

You shall not take the name of the Lord your God in vain.

Have you used the name of God as a curse or exclamation? Have you used the name of God, Jesus Christ, the Virgin Mary, or the saints in a way that detracts from faith or offends others? Have you used the name of God to coerce others to do your will? Have you sworn a false oath or lied, using God's name to prove your sincerity?

Remember the Sabbath day, to keep it holy.

Have you attended Mass on Sundays and holy days of obligation? Have you gone to Church for some purpose other than to worship God (e.g., to see and be seen, for the sake of looking good to friends or neighbors)? Do you participate in the Christian community and bring support, encouragement, and strength to your parish? Do you make a time of rest for yourself and those for whom you are responsible (e.g., family members, employees)?

Honor your father and your mother.

Have you shown due love, kindness, respect, and compassion to your parents? Are you willing to give encouragement and material assistance to your

parents? Are you respectful of all your family members, recognizing the bond you share? Do you show respect and due obedience to those in authority over you? Are you conscientious regarding your duties as a citizen? Do you support laws and public policies that strengthen the family? Are you respectful of all persons, no matter how close or distant the relationship?

You shall not kill.

Have you taken the life of another, or caused another to die? Have you participated in the act of abortion, infanticide, or euthanasia? Have you encouraged or enabled another to do so? Have you endangered the safety of others or yourself through the abuse of alcohol, drugs, or through the use of vehicles? Have you held hatred for another person? Have you willfully damaged the reputation of another? Have you ridiculed or insulted others? Have you led others into the practice of any sin?

You shall not commit adultery.

Have you engaged in sexual activity with someone other than your spouse? Do you respect the sanctity of marriage? Do you intentionally prevent the conception of children by artificial means? Do

you accept the goodness of sexuality, for yourself and others? Do you accept the value of chastity for all unmarried persons?

You shall not steal.

Have you taken possession of something that did not belong to you? Have you done damage to the property of another? Have you withheld money or property that is owed to another? Have you caused others to pay excessively for goods or services? Have you cheated another out of property, money, or rights? Have you gambled so as to risk being unable to provide for yourself and your family? Do you promote fair labor practices and just compensation? Do you give to the poor?

You shall not bear false witness against your neighbor.

Have you lied? Have you committed perjury by lying under oath? Have you damaged the reputation of another? Have you revealed negative facts about another without proper reason? Have you allowed another person to continue doing something wrong? Have you revealed secrets that have been told to you? Have you broken a professional standard of confidentiality in the workplace?

You shall not covet your neighbor's wife.

Do you lust after the spouse of another? Do you nurse feelings of sexual desire for someone who is not your spouse? Do you express lustful thoughts in the company of others? Do you use sexualized speech? Do you touch others or make gestures to satisfy sexual feelings? Do you use pornography? Do you masturbate? Have you failed to protect the sexual innocence of children? Do you appreciate the dignity of every person?

Do you recognize the value of your own sexual integrity?

You shall not covet your neighbor's goods.

Do you often wish you had what another has? Are you greedy, desiring more than you need? Do you have a desire to amass wealth and possessions without limit? Do you feel envious, becoming sad or frustrated at another's happiness or success? Do you wish harm or failure to someone who is more successful than you? Do you wish misfortune to another so that you will somehow profit? Do you seek the power that may accompany wealth?

Celebrating the Sacrament of Reconciliation

- ✛ Reflect and understand clearly how your behavior has damaged your relationship with God, the Church, and persons in your life.

- ✛ Begin with a Sign of the Cross and tell the priest how long it has been since your last confession.

- ✛ Tell the priest your sins.

- ✛ Listen for any words from him that may help you to deepen your faithfulness to Christ and to avoid repeating the sins.

- ✛ When the priest gives you a penance, indicate you understand it, or ask for clarification if you don't.

- ✛ Say an Act of Contrition (p. 9).

- ✛ Listen to the words of absolution.

- ✛ Complete your penance.

- ✛ Thank God for this great moment of grace in your life.

Prayerful Reading of Scripture (*Lectio Divina*)

For individual or group participation.

The practice of *Lectio Divina* introduces us to the power of the word in Scripture. It is an experience of attentive listening to the Lord who speaks to us in the depths of our hearts. We are invited to probe the spiritual meaning of the word and discover the fruits and challenges that Scripture hands to us, so that "the word of God is living and active" in our lives (see Heb 4:12).

Prepare the Environment

To create a prayerful atmosphere where you will practice *Lectio Divina*, arrange a table with a sacred image, a lighted candle, burning incense, and a green or flowering plant. Select a passage from Scripture, then take a reverent yet comfortable position and enter into a climate of silence, in an attitude of adoration. If *Lectio Divina* is carried out in a group, the one designated will guide the movement through the stages.

Lectio: Reading and Listening to the Word of God

Pray: Jesus, Divine Master, Son of the living God, teach me to listen to your word. Let me be attentive to what you want to tell me in this reading of holy Scripture, and let me discover your presence there.

Read the text of Scripture slowly, audibly, in order to engage your whole being: the body by using the lips to pronounce the words; the memory, which holds the words; the intelligence, which understands their meaning. The passage is read with the eyes of the heart, between the lines rather than along the lines. The reading should be done calmly and well, repeated several times. This reflective reading allows the Spirit to inspire a deeper understanding of the importance and meaning of certain phrases, no matter how familiar they may be. *Lectio* will bear fruit if, when reading the Scripture, you leave God completely free to make known what he wants you to contemplate.

Meditatio: Reflecting on the Word

Pray: Jesus, Divine Master, Son of the living God, teach me to assimilate your word so that it may transform me. Living Word, conform my spirit to become like you are and to welcome what you will for me.

Meditatio is a reflection on what has been read aloud, and harmonizes with the rhythm of the *lectio*. The intellect searches for the truth, centering on the text in order to discover its richness, not to outline applications to one's personal life. The mind lingers over a phrase that speaks more deeply to the heart. Here, give yourself over to the "taste" of Scripture through pondering and repetition. Repeat (aloud if in a group) the word or phrase that impresses you, or write it down and keep it in view.

Oratio: The Word Touches the Heart

Pray: Jesus, Divine Master, Son of the living God, teach me to speak to the Father. Fill my heart with the same love that unites you to the Father and the Holy Spirit. Word made flesh, pray in me and be my prayer to the Father.

Oratio is a sacred surrender of the heart to God, in order to offer him your sentiments of love and confidence. More than a raising of the heart to God, *oratio* is a descent of God to us. We provide him with a fitting vessel. The Word has come into the soul and now it returns to him under the form of prayer. The prayer that emerges is a simple, spontaneous prayer that is the fruit of the *lectio* and the *meditatio*.

Contemplatio: Entering the Silence

Pray: Jesus, Divine Master, Son of the living God, make my heart long for a love so great that your Spirit will give me a share in the communion of the love of the three divine Persons.

Contemplatio is a lifting up of the soul to God, the patient renunciation of one's resistance, a loving faithfulness in silent waiting. Keep silent and remain still, in deep recollection, re-entering into yourself in order to meet the One who is dwelling there. Silence takes the place of words. The soul waits in peaceful attentiveness to God.

Actio: Acting on the Word

Pray: Jesus, Divine Master, Son of the living God, be in me the fulfillment of the divine light received from Sacred Scripture. Word of God and God-with-us, grant that all I do and say may be a reflection of your love.

Actio makes the fruit of your *Lectio Divina* experience active in your life. What the Word has taught aligns the desires of your heart with the deeds of everyday living. The Word of God, which is "living and active," is to permeate one's whole life and being.

"If anyone loves me he will keep my word, and my Father will love him, and we will come to him and make our abode with him" (Jn 14:23).

Text Suggestions for *Lectio Divina*

You Are Salt and Light—Matthew 5:13–16

Practice Almsgiving—Matthew 6:1–4

Your Treasure—Matthew 6:19–21

The Sower—Mark 4:1–6

Calming of the Storm—Mark 4:35–41

Jesus' Invitation—Mark 8:34–38

Courage—Luke 12:4–7

CATHOLIC BELIEFS AND PRACTICES

The Ten Commandments of God

The Decalogue is made known to us by divine Revelation, that is, through Sacred Scripture, and expresses how we are to act in order to respond to God's unconditional love for us. The Ten Commandments are expressions of the natural law that is written on our hearts, and they affirm the obligations we have toward God and one another. The first three commandments point out the way we are to love God; the other seven, how we are to love our neighbor.

I am the Lord your God:

1. You shall not have other gods besides me.
2. You shall not take the name of the Lord your God in vain.
3. Remember to keep holy the Lord's day.
4. Honor your father and your mother.
5. You shall not kill.

6. You shall not commit adultery.

7. You shall not steal.

8. You shall not bear false witness against your neighbor.

9. You shall not covet your neighbor's wife.

10. You shall not covet your neighbor's goods (see Ex 20:1–17).

THE TWO GREAT COMMANDMENTS

When asked which of the commandments was the most important, Jesus summed them up in these words:

"'You shall love the Lord with all your heart and with all your soul and with all your understanding; this is the first and greatest commandment. And the second is like it. 'You shall love your neighbor as yourself'" (Mt 22:37–40).

THE SEVEN SACRAMENTS

The sacraments are actions of Jesus, sacred signs through which Jesus gives us his Spirit and makes his people holy by grace. Each sacrament gives us a particular grace, and through each sacrament the Holy Spirit transforms us and unites us to Christ. The sacraments touch each of the important moments of our spiritual journey through life.

Baptism	Anointing of the Sick
Confirmation	Holy Orders
Holy Eucharist	Matrimony
Reconciliation	

Special Duties of Catholics: The Precepts of the Church

The precepts of the Church are special duties that Catholics are expected to obey and fulfill. They set down certain acts of religion and penance in order to apply the commandments of God and the teachings of the Gospel to the lives of the faithful.

1. To worship God by participating in Mass every Sunday and holy day of obligation in order to keep holy the day of the Lord's resurrection, and to rest from servile labor on these days.

2. To receive the sacrament of Reconciliation at least once a year; this continues the work of conversion in preparation for reception of the Eucharist.

3. To receive Holy Communion during the Easter Season (in the United States and Canada, this duty may be fulfilled between the

First Sunday of Lent to Trinity Sunday); this guarantees reception of the Body and Blood of the Lord at the Paschal time, which is the heart of the Church's liturgy.

4. To observe the days of fasting and abstinence established by the Church. These penitential acts prepare us for the feasts of the liturgical year, as well as strengthen us spiritually.

5. To help to provide for the needs of the Church. This means that the faithful are to assist with the material needs of the Church, according to their ability.

THE BEATITUDES

The Beatitudes are the heart of Jesus' teaching. They describe both our attitude as disciples of Christ and the promises of the kingdom, offering us concrete ways to conform our life to the life and teachings of Christ. The Beatitudes express our natural desire for happiness and, at the same time, they challenge us to conform all our choices to the teachings of Jesus Christ. Living as his disciples should be our one true concern and the guiding principle in all our actions.

> Blessed are the poor in spirit, for theirs is the kingdom of heaven.
>
> Blessed are those who mourn, for they shall be comforted.
>
> Blessed are the meek, for they shall inherit the earth.
>
> Blessed are those who hunger and thirst to do God's will, for they shall have their fill.

Blessed are the merciful, for they shall receive
mercy.

Blessed are the pure of heart, for they shall see
God.

Blessed are the peacemakers, for they shall be
called sons of God.

Blessed are those who are persecuted for
doing God's will, for theirs is the kingdom
of heaven.

Blessed are you when they insult you and
persecute you and say every sort of evil thing
against you on account of me; rejoice and be
glad, because your reward will be great in
heaven—they persecuted the prophets before
you in the same way (Mt 5:3–12).

THE WORKS OF MERCY

The works of mercy are unselfish acts by which we help those who are in need. The spiritual works of mercy are directed toward caring for people's spiritual need. The corporal works of mercy are directed toward providing for the basic bodily needs of people. By practicing the works of mercy we fulfill Jesus' command to love our neighbor as he loves us.

Spiritual Works

1. To admonish the sinner
2. To instruct the ignorant
3. To counsel the doubtful
4. To comfort the sorrowful
5. To bear wrongs patiently
6. To forgive injuries
7. To pray for the living and the dead

Corporal Works

1. To feed the hungry
2. To give drink to the thirsty
3. To clothe the naked
4. To shelter the homeless
5. To visit the sick
6. To visit the imprisoned
7. To bury the dead

The Virtues

The Theological Virtues

The theological virtues have God as their origin, motive, and object. God gives them to us so that we might direct our whole life to him.

Faith   Hope   Love

The Cardinal Virtues

The cardinal virtues are the key moral virtues—dispositions, attitudes, and habits of behaving in an upright way. They are strengths of character developed by personal effort that enable a person to live with freedom and self-control. Divine grace purifies and elevates them.

Prudence   Fortitude
Justice   Temperance

The Gifts of the Holy Spirit

The gifts of the Holy Spirit prepare us to receive grace and make it easier to practice virtues, and they motivate us to be receptive to the inspirations of the Holy Spirit.

Wisdom

Understanding

Counsel (right judgment)

Fortitude (courage)

Knowledge

Piety (love)

Fear of the Lord (reverence)

THE FRUITS OF THE HOLY SPIRIT

The fruits of the Holy Spirit are good deeds and habits that result from our response to the Holy Spirit's inspirations to do good.

Charity	Patience
Long-suffering	Modesty
Joy	Kindness
Humility	Continence
Peace	Goodness
Fidelity	Chastity

Holy Days of Obligation

Besides all Sundays of the year, canon law specifies ten holy days of obligation, but allows the bishops of each country to determine if they will be observed as holy days of obligation.

Holy Days of Obligation in the United States

January 1	Solemnity of Mary, Mother of God
Forty days after Easter, or in some dioceses, the following Sunday	Ascension of our Lord
August 15	Assumption of the Blessed Virgin Mary
November 1	All Saints' Day

December 8	Immaculate Conception of Mary
December 25	Christmas Day

Christmas is always a holy day of obligation on whatever day of the week it falls. When the feasts of the Assumption, All Saints, or the Solemnity of Mary, Mother of God (January 1) are celebrated on a Saturday or Monday, there is no obligation to participate in Mass. The Immaculate Conception remains a holy day of obligation except when December 8 falls on Sunday. Then the feast is transferred to Monday, in which case it is not considered a holy day. However, the faithful are still encouraged to participate at Mass on these days.

The other holy days specified in canon law for the universal Church are: Epiphany, Corpus Christi (The Body and Blood of the Lord), the feasts of Saint Joseph (March 19) and the Apostles Peter and Paul (June 29).

Holy Days of Obligation in Canada

December 25	Christmas Day
January 1	Feast of Mary, Mother of God
Epiphany, Ascension of the Lord, and Corpus Christi are transferred to the following Sunday.	

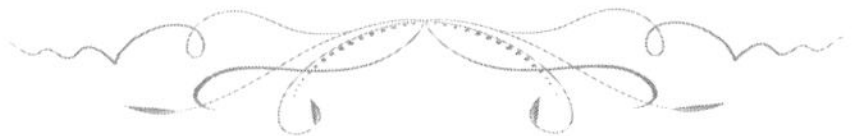

DAYS OF FAST AND ABSTINENCE

The words of Jesus: "If anyone would be my disciple, he must deny himself, and take up his cross daily and follow me" (Lk 9:23), are not just an invitation. All Christians are required to perform acts of penance through fasting, prayer, and almsgiving. So that all Catholics may be joined in a common observance of penance, penitential days are prescribed in which the faithful pray, perform good works, deny themselves by fulfilling their responsibilities more faithfully, and observe fast and abstinence.

A fast day is a day in which only one full meal is taken; the other two meals together should not equal a full meal. Eating between meals is not permitted, but liquids, including milk and fruit juices, are allowed. Catholics who have reached the age of eighteen but are not yet fifty-nine are obliged to fast.

In the United States and Canada, the only fast days are:

Ash Wednesday
Good Friday.

A day of abstinence means refraining from eating meat on certain "days of abstinence" specified by the Church. Catholics fourteen years of age and over are obliged to keep this law.

In the United States the days for abstinence from meat are:

Ash Wednesday
All Fridays of Lent
Good Friday.

In Canada the days for abstinence from meat are:

Ash Wednesday
Good Friday.

All other Fridays, including the Fridays of Lent, are days of abstinence, but Catholics may substitute abstinence with some other act of piety or charity. Catholics fourteen years of age and over are obliged to keep this law.

The Eucharistic Fast

A person who receives Holy Communion should do so with faith, reverence, and love. Catholics must believe that Jesus is really present in the Holy Eucharist, be free from serious sin, and observe the fast before receiving Communion.

We are required to fast for one hour from all solid foods and liquids, both alcoholic and non-alcoholic (with the exception of water, which can be taken at any time, and medicine).

The elderly and the ill, as well as those who care for them, need only fast for fifteen minutes before receiving Communion.

Catholics should receive Communion at least once a year (usually between the first Sunday in Lent and Trinity Sunday). This is known as the Easter duty.

Reception of Communion
by Non-Catholics

The Eucharist is the premier sign of our unity in Christ; receiving Communion testifies to unity of faith and worship. For this reason, the Catholic Church cannot invite non-Catholics to receive Communion, since they do not share the same faith. In certain circumstances, however, the bishop may permit some other Christians to receive Communion if they truly believe what Catholics do about the Sacrament and sincerely ask for it.

ACKNOWLEDGMENTS

Old Testament Scripture quotations contained herein are from the *New Revised Standard Version Bible: Catholic Edition,* copyright © 1989, 1993, Division of Christian Education of the National Council of the Churches of Christ in the United States of America. Used by permission. All rights reserved.

New Testament Scripture quotations contained herein are from the *The New Testament: St. Paul Catholic Edition,* translated by Mark A. Wauck, copyright © 2000 by the Society of St. Paul, Staten Island, New York, and are used by permission. All rights reserved.

Quotations from the book of Psalms are taken from *The Psalms: A Translation from the Hebrew,* translated by Miguel Miguens, copyright © 1995, Daughters of St. Paul. All rights reserved.

Excerpts from *Preparation for the Sacrament of Reconciliation,* copyright © 2000, Daughters of St. Paul. All rights reserved.

Prayers from Saint Faustina's diary are taken from *Jesus, I Trust in You,* copyright © 2003, Daughters of St. Paul. All rights reserved.

The English translation of Angelus from *A Book of Prayers,* © 1982, International Commission on English in the Liturgy Corporation (ICEL); the English translation of the Apostles' Creed from *The Roman Missal*, © 2010, ICEL. All rights reserved.

English translation of Glory by the International Consultation on English Texts (ICET).

The English translation of Pope Francis's prayer: To Mary, Untier of Knots, copyright © Libreria Editrice Vaticana. Used with permission.

The Night Litany, copyright © The Carmelite Monastery, Philadelphia, PA. Used with permission.

All other prayers were taken from common sources.

ART PIECES:

Page xvi   Jean-François Millet. *L'Angélus* (*The Angelus*), 1857–1859. RMN-Grand Palais, Musèe d'Orsay. http://commons.wikimedia.org/wiki/File:Jean-Fran%C3%A7ois_Millet_-_The_Angelus_-_Google_Art_Project.jpg.

Page 14   Albrecht Dürer. *Allerheiligenbild* (*The Adoration of the Trinity*), 1511. Kunsthistorisches Museum. http://commons.wikimedia.org/wiki/File:Albrecht_D%C3%BCrer_-_Adoration_of_the_Trinity_%28Landauer_Altar%29_-_Google_Art_Project.jpg.

Page 22   Piero di Cosimo. *The Incarnation of Jesus* (also known as *The Immaculate Conception with Saints*), 1495–1505. Uffizi Museum. http://commons.wikimedia.org/wiki/File:Piero_di_Cosimo_057.jpg.

Page 34   Henrich Hofmann. *Christ and the Rich Young Ruler* (detail), c. 1889. Riverside Church. http://commons.wikimedia.org/wiki/File:Christ,_by_Heinrich_Hofmann.jpg.

Page 78   Lucas Cranach the Elder. *Madonna mit Kind* (Madonna and Child), c. 1518. Staatliche Kunsthalle Karlsruhe. http://commons.wikimedia.org/wiki/File:Lucas_Cranach_d.%C3%84._-_Madonna_mit_Kind_%28Karlsruhe,_Kunsthalle%29.jpg.

Page 122   Francesco Botticini. *I Tre Arcangeli e Tobias* (Three Archangels with Tobias), c. 1470. Uffizi Museum. http://commons.wikimedia.org/wiki/File:Francesco_Botticini_-_I_tre_Arcangeli_e_Tobias.jpg.

Page 136   Giovanni di Paolo. *Paradise*, mid-fifteenth century. Metropolitan Museum of Art. http://commons.wikimedia.org/wiki/File:Giovanni_di_Paolo_003.jpg.

Page 214   Bartolomé Estéban Murillo. *The Virgin of the Rosary*, 1675–80. Dulwich Picture Gallery. http://commons.wikimedia.org/wiki/File:Murillo,_Bartolom%C3%A9_Est%C3%A9ban_-_The_Madonna_of_the_Rosary_-_Google_Art_Project.jpg.

Page 232   Philippe de Champaigne. *Jesus the Good Shepherd*, 1650–60. Palais des Beaux-Arts de Lille. http://commons.wikimedia.org/wiki/File:Champaigne_shepherd.jpg.

Page 274   Sandro Botticelli. *Madonna and Child*, ca. 1479. Museo Poldi Pezzoli, Milan, Italy. http://upload.

wikimedia.org/wikipedia/commons/8/8a/Sandro_
Botticelli_065.jpg.

Page 284   Carl Heinrich Bloch. *The Sermon on the Mount*, 1871.
The Museum of National History at Frederiks-
borg Castle. http://commons.wikimedia.org/wiki/
File:Bloch-SermonOnTheMount.jpg.

Page 302   Pietro Perugino. *Baptism of Christ* (detail), c. 1482.
Sistine Chapel. http://commons.wikimedia.org/wiki/
File:Perugino,_battesimo_di_cristo_02.jpg.

LIST OF CONTRIBUTORS

INDEX

BOOKS & MEDIA

A mission of the Daughters of St. Paul

As apostles of Jesus Christ,
evangelizing today's world:

We are CALLED to holiness
by God's living Word and Eucharist.

We COMMUNICATE the Gospel message
through our lives and through all
available forms of media.

We SERVE the Church
by responding to the hopes and needs
of all people with the Word of God,
in the spirit of St. Paul.

For more information visit our website:
www.pauline.org.